The Land and People of
TANZANIA

The United Republic of Tanzania was formed in 1964 from the former independent republics of Tanganyika and Zanzibar. This land was one of mankind's earliest homes; archaeologists have found evidence of human habitation dating back a million years. Within the past decade, Tanzania has made rapid strides into the modern world with such innovations as the Tanzara Railway Project and a new form of social and economic organization, the ujamaa village.

In this newly revised edition, the author traces Tanzania's recent social and economic progress and describes the republic's role in the African community and in world affairs.

PORTRAITS OF THE NATIONS SERIES

THE LAND AND PEOPLE OF AFGHANISTAN

THE LAND AND PEOPLE OF ALGERIA

THE LAND AND PEOPLE OF ARGENTINA

THE LAND AND PEOPLE OF AUSTRALIA

THE LAND AND PEOPLE OF AUSTRIA

THE LAND AND PEOPLE OF THE BALKANS

THE LAND AND PEOPLE OF BELGIUM

THE LAND AND PEOPLE OF BRAZIL

THE LAND AND PEOPLE OF BURMA

THE LAND AND PEOPLE OF CAMBODIA

THE LAND AND PEOPLE OF CANADA

THE LAND AND PEOPLE OF CENTRAL AMERICA

THE LAND AND PEOPLE OF CEYLON

THE LAND AND PEOPLE OF CHILE

THE LAND AND PEOPLE OF CHINA

THE LAND AND PEOPLE OF COLOMBIA

THE LAND AND PEOPLE OF THE CONGO

THE LAND AND PEOPLE OF CZECHOSLOVAKIA

THE LAND AND PEOPLE OF DENMARK

THE LAND AND PEOPLE OF EGYPT

THE LAND AND PEOPLE OF ENGLAND

THE LAND AND PEOPLE OF ETHIOPIA

THE LAND AND PEOPLE OF FINLAND

THE LAND AND PEOPLE OF FRANCE

THE LAND AND PEOPLE OF GERMANY

THE LAND AND PEOPLE OF GHANA

THE LAND AND PEOPLE OF GREECE

THE LAND AND PEOPLE OF THE GUIANAS

THE LAND AND PEOPLE OF HOLLAND

THE LAND AND PEOPLE OF HUNGARY

THE LAND AND PEOPLE OF ICELAND

THE LAND AND PEOPLE OF INDIA

THE LAND AND PEOPLE OF INDONESIA

THE LAND AND PEOPLE OF IRAN

THE LAND AND PEOPLE OF IRAQ

THE LAND AND PEOPLE OF IRELAND

THE LAND AND PEOPLE OF ISRAEL

THE LAND AND PEOPLE OF ITALY

THE LAND AND PEOPLE OF JAPAN

THE LAND AND PEOPLE OF JORDAN

THE LAND AND PEOPLE OF KENYA

THE LAND AND PEOPLE OF KOREA

THE LAND AND PEOPLE OF LEBANON

THE LAND AND PEOPLE OF LIBERIA

THE LAND AND PEOPLE OF LIBYA

THE LAND AND PEOPLE OF MALAYSIA

THE LAND AND PEOPLE OF MEXICO

THE LAND AND PEOPLE OF MOROCCO

THE LAND AND PEOPLE OF NEW ZEALAND

THE LAND AND PEOPLE OF NIGERIA

THE LAND AND PEOPLE OF NORWAY

THE LAND AND PEOPLE OF PAKISTAN

THE LAND AND PEOPLE OF PERU

THE LAND AND PEOPLE OF THE PHILIPPINES

THE LAND AND PEOPLE OF POLAND

THE LAND AND PEOPLE OF PORTUGAL

THE LAND AND PEOPLE OF RHODESIA

THE LAND AND PEOPLE OF ROMANIA

THE LAND AND PEOPLE OF RUSSIA

THE LAND AND PEOPLE OF SCOTLAND

THE LAND AND PEOPLE OF SOUTH AFRICA

THE LAND AND PEOPLE OF SPAIN

THE LAND AND PEOPLE OF SWEDEN

THE LAND AND PEOPLE OF SWITZERLAND

THE LAND AND PEOPLE OF SYRIA

THE LAND AND PEOPLE OF TANZANIA

THE LAND AND PEOPLE OF THAILAND

THE LAND AND PEOPLE OF TUNISIA

THE LAND AND PEOPLE OF TURKEY

THE LAND AND PEOPLE OF URUGUAY

THE LAND AND PEOPLE OF VENEZUELA

THE LAND AND PEOPLE OF THE WEST INDIES

Also in the same format

THE ISLANDS OF HAWAII

THE ISLAND OF PUERTO RICO

The Land and People of
TANZANIA

by Edna Mason Kaula

PORTRAITS OF THE NATIONS SERIES

J. B. LIPPINCOTT COMPANY
Philadelphia   New York

The author is most grateful to the Tanzania Mission to the United Nations for their permission to reproduce the photographs that appear in this book.

U.S. Library of Congress Cataloging in Publication Data

Kaula, Edna Mason.
 The land and people of Tanzania.

 (Portraits of the nations series)
 SUMMARY: An introduction to the geography, history, people, industries, culture, and social progress of the largest country in East Africa.

 1. Tanzania—Juvenile literature. [1. Tanzania] I. Title.
DT438.K33   916.78   72-5660
ISBN-0-397-31270-9   ISBN-0-397-31410-8 (lib. bdg.)

For Asha, Paul, and David Confer

Contents

1   A Land Without Winter   11

2   Tanzania's People   20

3   The President and TANU   31

4   The Island of Cloves   40

5   The President and Foreign Aid   47

6   The Arusha Declaration   51

7   Ujamaa Villages   56

8   The War Against Ignorance   65

9   Prevention and Cure   72

10 Transportation   78

11 Industry   86

12 Natural Resources   94

13 Artists and Their Works   98

14 Beyond the Cities   106

15 The East African Community   119

16 The President Speaks   128

    Index   135

The Land and People of
TANZANIA

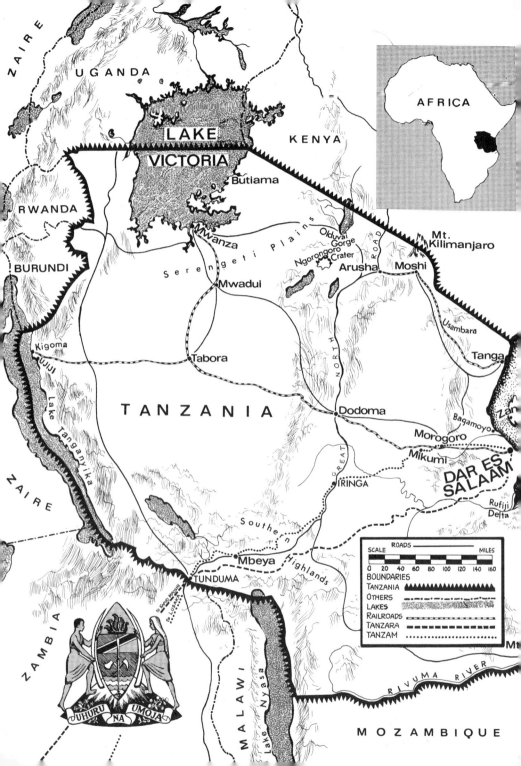

1

A Land Without Winter

The United Republic of Tanzania is the largest country in East Africa. It covers 362,820 square miles—an area that equals a combined Florida, Louisiana, and Texas. Contained within Tanzanian borders is natural scenery unrivaled anywhere for variety and beauty. One sees beauty in the sharp silhouette of high mountains against a clear blue sky, in the purple shadows of deep valleys and the golden light that shimmers over wide, flat plains. There is beauty in the stillness of impenetrable, misty swamps and the dappled green light reflected in Tanzania's lakes. Zanzibar and Pemba, offshore islands that are included in the republic, have beauty in the richness of luxuriant vegetation competing for a place in the tropical sun.

Sunrise comes to this new nation's five-hundred-mile-long coastline across the Indian Ocean. Its rays climb an incline that starts from ten to forty miles inland from the ocean and runs the length of Tanzania. They strike the tall, gleaming peak of Mount Kilimanjaro before they touch the intermediate highlands. Kilimanjaro rises to a height of 19,340 feet above lush, tropical foliage. It is Africa's highest mountain and, though a mere five degrees south of the equator, is capped with perpetual snow.

Mount Kilimanjaro's twin peaks, Kibo (*foreground*) and Mawenzi.

Just north and to the west of Kilimanjaro lies Lake Victoria, 3,720 feet above sea level and Africa's largest lake. Tanzania shares the lake with Kenya and Uganda. Other neighboring countries are Ruanda, Burundi, and Zaire, formerly the Congo, which is separated from Tanzania by Lake Tanganyika, the world's second deepest lake. Bordering Tanzania to the south are Zambia, Malawi, Lake Nyasa, and Mozambique.

The steep drop from the highlands to the coastal strip acts as a deterrent to navigation and during the descent most of Tanzania's rivers turn into rapids. But three great African rivers, the White Nile, the Congo, and the Zambezi, are fed by the Tanzanian watershed.

Being wholly within the tropics makes Tanzania a land without winter. Temperatures depend upon altitudes. The climate varies from intense heat and humidity along the coastal strip to a wider temperature range and less humidity at altitudes up to two thousand feet. Over the central plateau, which lies between the Great Rift valley's two forks and averages three thousand to four thousand feet in altitude, the climate is still hot but dry. But in the semitemperate mountain regions, up to six thousand feet, the days are cool and the nights are cold and invigorating. By comparison, both Pemba and Zanzibar, being located at sea level, are hot and humid.

Tanzania's climate substitutes summers and winters with definite wet and dry seasons. From November to April or May the northeast monsoons (or winds) bring rain. Soon, the plains are ablaze with colorful wild flowers. Trees sprout new leaves and farm crops flourish. When the monsoons reverse their direction, and blow from the southwest, abundant growth ceases and the land lies dormant.

Tanganyika, as it was called until recently, was the first country in East Africa to win independence from foreign rule. In May of the year 1961 and after many years of striving for *Uhuru*—"Freedom"—Tanganyikans won internal self-government. At last, the people were relieved of the United Nations Trusteeship that Great Britain had administered since 1946. On the night of Uhuru, every Tanganyikan man, woman, and child throughout the land danced and cheered as demonstrations of their great happiness. Even in the smallest villages the people lit huge

bonfires, and from high on the mountaintops they shot spectacular rockets that brightened the sky in a wide radius.

On December 9, 1962, Tanganyika became a republic within
the British Commonwealth of Nations. Two years later, on January 12, 1964, the United Republic of Tanzania (pronounced

President Nyerere (*left, standing*) addresses his guests at a state dinner in
commemoration of Tanzania's tenth independence anniversary.

Tan-zan-EEE-a) was formed when Tanganyika and the islands, Pemba and Zanzibar, became one nation. The two islands, important to East Africa's development, lie within twenty-five miles of the mainland coast.

The harbor of Zanzibar, the main town on the island, is one of the nation's four. In addition, there are three large lake ports. Fifty-four airfields are used as inland connecting points where roads are poor or nonexistent.

Tanzania is primarily an agricultural country. Such a large land, boasting the extremes of great heights and awesome depths, allows for the growing of a wide variety of crops on a year-round basis if properly and scientifically tended. But before these ideal conditions could be attained there were many problems to overcome.

Tanzania's leaders saw that the age-old system of subsistence farming would have to be replaced with modern methods of cultivation if their country was to be independent in the fullest sense. Flood and drought control, the eradication of insect pests, diseases, and illiteracy were among necessary items in the education program they planned. Tanzania's terrain had to be considered also. With right treatment, Tanzania's good soil could be made to yield more abundant and superior crops in the right places at the right time. The planners faced a formidable task. The increased production they anticipated reaping must have easy access to marketing centers. New roads would have to be built that led to new trading centers.

Dar es Salaam, a cosmopolitan city and Tanzania's capital, was by far the biggest at the time of independence. Eight years later it was still the biggest city with a population, in 1970, of over 250,000. Situated beside a magnificent harbor and adjacent to easy transportation, the city acted like a magnet to new business ventures and industries, as a comfortable place to live in and the likeliest spot to reap a fortune. While other Tanzanian towns languished, Dar es Salaam continued to expand.

Decentralizing commerce by selecting nine towns for concentrated urban development was not the first project undertaken by the new government, but it served to weld the country into one vast unit of activity.

To lure commerce from Dar es Salaam, each of the nine chosen towns was conveniently situated as an outlet for specialized

Dar es Salaam, a section of the city and harbor.

Members of the Mbwa Maji Fishing Society in Dar es Salaam.

products, a condition that attracts other activities such as workshops and small industries.

Second in size to Dar es Salaam is Tanga, a seaport to the north and the center of the sisal industry; Tanzania is the biggest producer of sisal in the world. Tanga is the rail terminal to which diesel-engined freight trains bring the produce from the rich northern provinces and return to the highlands with machinery and other imported items. The train pulls into Moshi, located near the slopes of Mount Kilimanjaro where coffee is grown. The coffee is brought into Moshi's auction rooms, then processed. Moshi is also active with sugar refineries. In Arusha, at the end of the line, small industries such as the manufacturing of automobile tires thrive. It is in Arusha that the secretariat of a newly formed East African Community has its headquarters where officials from Kenya, Tanzania, and Uganda meet in conference. From high, cool Arusha safaris set out to view Tanzania's bountiful wildlife. The town has the distinction, also, of being centered exactly midway between Cairo and Cape Town.

On the southern railroad, Morogoro, a center for education and industries like bicycle manufacturing, is one of the chosen towns along with Dodoma which lies on the hot central plain but at a crossroads with the Great North Road, a link joining North and South Africa. Farther inland, selected towns are Tabora at a railroad junction leading to Lake Tanganyika, and at the end of the line beside Lake Victoria, Mwanza, the center of successful cotton-growing and textile industries.

A new road under construction from Dar es Salaam to Lusaka in Zambia passes through Mbeya in the Southern Highlands. The ninth town chosen for urban development is Mtwara in Tanzania's southeast corner. Mtwara is in the heart of the cashew-growing and processing area, an industry in which Tanzania is second only to Mozambique in world production.

As the experiment in land and town development progresses, other centers will be considered for similar programs.

Prior to independence Tanzania was classed as a severely underdeveloped land, but its story today is one of unprecedented growth. With encouragement and gentle persuasion, Tanzania's leaders have awakened in the people a driving ambition to succeed as nation-builders. With such a united people, dedicated to learning and to hard work, Tanzania is well on the way to being economically independent.

2

Tanzania's People

When independence came to Tanzania many people expected Uhuru to mean that the luxuries of life were to be theirs free. The real truth soon became apparent—that freedom with its material benefits is the reward of hard work. Tanzanians responded enthusiastically to the awesome task of nation-building, following the advice of their instructors and combining their efforts toward future achievements. Even the smallest children were oriented for national service.

Of Tanzania's almost 13 million inhabitants, the great majority of mainland Tanzanians are Africans, 95 percent of whom live in rural areas with about 90 percent working on the land. The country's population also includes approximately twenty-five thousand Arabs, eighty thousand Asians of Indian origin, and fifteen thousand Europeans. On the two adjacent islands there are approximately three hundred thousand Africans, fifty thousand Arabs, and twenty thousand Asians. Of these numbers, 55 percent live on Zanzibar and 45 percent on Pemba.

Among Tanzania's Arab residents are descendants of traders who were in command of East Africa's coastal regions from the

Schoolchildren entertaining President Nyerere during visit to Kibondo.

sixth to the sixteenth century. They brought luxury items such as jewels and cloth which they exchanged for ivory and rhinoceros horn. The profitable business included slave-trading, and a well-trodden slave route extended inland from Bagamoyo on the coast to Ujiji, a trading center on the east shore of Lake Tanganyika.

Women of the Makonde tribe wearing traditional lip plugs.

As evidence of Arab affluence there are old but imposing buildings, decorated lavishly with Oriental furnishings and tapestries,
still standing in coastal towns. Arab glory ended with the con-
quest by Portuguese explorers, but those Arabs who maintained
permanent homes, or who had married African women, remained in Africa.

The Swahili language evolved from this mingling by marriage
of Arabs to African women. Now Tanzania's official language,
along with English, and the most widely spoken in East Africa

and extending into Central Africa, Swahili has borrowed words from Arabic, English, and Portuguese vocabularies.

Some of the Indians in Tanzania are three or four generations removed from the thirty-seven thousand laborers the British brought from India in 1900 as construction workers on a railroad through Kenya. Other Indians came to Tanzania as retailers in small goods. They were probably the first non-Africans to penetrate the farthest corners of Tanzania's back country where they introduced previously unknown and exciting articles like woven cloth, knives, lamps, and matches to people who lead simple lives in isolated villages.

Though little was known of Tanzania's interior until 1857, when Sir Richard Burton and John Speke set out in a search for the source of the Nile River, it has been occupied by man for a long time.

Scientists call East Africa the "cradle of mankind," for in 1959

Sukuma girl carrying water.

Dr. and Mrs. L. S. B. Leakey found the fossil skull of *Zinjanthropus*, the then earliest known hominid. Dr. Leakey is a Kenya-born anthropologist of British parentage, and in 1959 was curator of the Corydon Museum in Nairobi, Kenya. He and his wife were digging three hundred feet down in Olduvai, a narrow rocky gorge in northern Tanzania, when, in the lowest layer of the gorge's wall, they came across the fossils. *Zinjanthropus's* age of about 1,750,000 years was determined by the argon method of measuring the radioactive form of carbon called carbon 14. Carbon 14 is formed in the atmosphere by cosmic rays and all living things take the element in when eating or breathing. While alive they maintain a fixed, known carbon 14 concentration, but when they die the concentration drops as the radioactive material decays. By measuring how much of the original carbon 14 concentration had decayed in the ancient skull, its age was determined. The "Nutcracker Man," as the skull was nicknamed because of its large teeth, now reposes in the national museum in Dar es Salaam.

Tanzania is fortunate that her African residents have on the whole evolved from the same source, a condition that minimizes the danger of internal racial dissensions such as have occurred in other newly emerged African nations. They belong to the widespread Bantu-speaking ethnic group that accounts for two-thirds of all Africans and they inhabit most of Africa south of the equator.

Some two thousand years ago Negroid ancestors of today's Tanzanians commenced a series of migrations from their original homeland, possibly the Niger River Delta. Always traveling in an easterly direction, this great movement of people was spread over hundreds of years. It ended in the Great Lakes Region,

.mainly along the shores of Lake Victoria. There the newcomers, divided into separate tribes, worked as farmers in the rich, productive soil. Other groups were also on the move. Nilotic tribespeople from the Sudan were pouring into the area. Hamites came from the northeast. The three groups met and from their mingling and intermarrying emerged distinctive new types of individuals. They were the Bantu. In at least five hundred dialects of the Bantu language, the word *Bantu* means "persons" with *Muntu* the singular form.

In time the Great Lakes area became so congested with settlers that there was hardly land enough for a farmer to sow his grain. (The Lake Victoria region is still the most densely populated in East Africa.) Not only was the region crowded with humans, but the cattle introduced by the Hamites took up a lot of space with their grazing. The Bantu quickly learned to become cattle herders as well as farmers, and the possession of many head of cattle, regardless of quality, became indicative of a man's wealth.

It was time to move on when the cattle started multiplying faster than the human occupants, so a number of Bantu tribes started south into previously unknown pastures. They drove their precious cattle before them as they wandered up and down and across central and southern Africa seeking new permanent homes. Eventually, about 120 different Bantu tribes settled down in the land that is now Tanzania. The largest Bantu tribal group in Tanzania are the Sukuma who number approximately one million. Their home, Sukumaland, covers a wide area south of Lake Victoria.

Life in the new environment followed the centuries-old traditional pattern. A paramount chief presided over each tribal group which was divided into self-contained units, the largest under the supervision of chiefs, the smaller under the control of headmen.

The villagers observed countless laws and taboos, important among them being a respect for ancestor spirits which the Bantu believed were very much part of their everyday life. Essentially animists, Tanzania's first residents appeased the spirits with special ceremonies that required the strictest discipline, and which strengthened the kinship ties that are stronger by far than any in Western society. (Today, more than three million Tanzanians ob-

Presidential launch arrives at Mwangongo village on the shores of Lake Tanganyika during president's visit.

serve the Islamic faith which was introduced by the Arabs and, since the coming of missionaries in the mid-eighteenth century, two and one-half million follow Christianity.)

Though a few Bantu tribes built their houses, or *nyumbas,* as squares or rectangles, the majority erected small round houses of mud and clay and thatched them with long pieces of grass laced with hemp strands against the wind. They used mud and clay for flooring, pounding the mixture into a tight mass, then polishing the floor with a rounded stone so that it shone like glass. The smoke from the small fires within the nyumbas seeped through the thatch, no provision ever being made for chimneys or windows.

Villagers seldom found reasons for leaving their farms, or *shambas,* in the old days. But when Europeans came to Tanzania they lured young men from the villages to be workers on large sisal and coffee estates, or in the mines. There was prestige value in working away from home, then returning after a time with gifts bought in an estate's general store.

Every member of a family helped with the farm work. They utilized the land around them for growing just enough foodstuffs for their own use. The men turned the soil with hoes called *jembes,* the women sowed the seeds of millet and yams. Year after year the farmers planted with no thought of replacing the goodness they reaped from the soil. Farmers were forced to move to fresh land after about three seasons for by that time the earth was worked out and devastating erosion resulted. The abused soil needed at least fifteen years to recover its lost richness. This was the general practice in farming throughout Tanzania.

As keepers of cattle only, the Nilo-Hamitic tribesmen fashioned spears for killing lions rather than making hoes for growing

A sisal plantation.

food. The Masai, who were the most prominent of the Hamitic tribes, were satisfied with drinking milk and blood taken from their cattle for sustenance. But the sharp hooves of their thousands of head of cattle, for they believed the slaughter of an animal was criminal, ground the soil into dust and ruined the land even more drastically than did the farmers' method of shifting cultivation.

In the past few years the land shortage reached a crisis in Tanzania. Europeans having introduced modern medical services, first by missionaries then by government agencies, it was easy to see that the resulting increased population would be demanding more and more arable land if people were to survive.

Tanzania's peasant farmers needed to learn to respect and value the land they occupied. They had also to learn to ade- ⟩ →

President Nyerere beats traditional drum in Dar es Salaam to signify start of tenth independence anniversary celebrations.

quately protect themselves against flood, drought, and fire. In short, the farmers needed to learn to conscientiously practice modern farming methods. The methods were available. How to bring them to people scattered into the remotest corners of Tanzania was the problem.

Who could teach them? It was Tanzania's good fortune that a leader emerged who possessed a gift for organization. He set the spark that ignited an ambition in the people to better their lives, and he provided them with the knowledge that a happier condition could be reached only by the force of individual effort.

3

The President and TANU

During the year 1922 a son was born to one wife of Nyerere Burite, chief of the Wazanaki tribe and already the father of twenty-five sons. The parents named the baby Julius Kambarage Nyerere. As they watched him as a toddler playing around their village of Butiama near Lake Victoria, they hardly suspected that Julius was destined to one day win freedom from colonialism for their country and that he would be their forward-looking president. The story of Tanzania's development is also that of Julius Nyerere. The man and nation are irrevocably welded.

As a small boy Julius was quick to answer correctly the riddles asked him by his mother, the traditional method of starting a child's education.

If she asked, "Which thin, shining spears touch earth and heaven at the same time?" the boy would answer, "Rainfall."

A second riddle example of a more personal nature is, "You have two sisters and two brothers whom you can never see." And the answer is, "My ears and eyes."

Traditional also were his duties of watching the sheep and goats and, when of a more responsible age, of herding cattle.

Julius Nyerere received his first formal education at a small Catholic missionary school near his home. Later he attended a Catholic missionary school at Tabora.

The experience of seeing white people and automobiles for the first time and the treasures he discovered between the covers of books opened a new, thrilling world for the impressionable boy. Julius became a diligent student and made good grades, though according to the records he "resisted discipline."

Julius was drawn to the mission school's religion and while at Tabora he adopted Roman Catholicism, a faith he still practices.

At Makerere University College, in Uganda, Julius won first prize in a literary competition, choosing for his subject "An application of John Mill's arguments for feminism as applied to the tribal societies of Tanganyika." When, in 1946, he graduated from Makerere he took a teacher's diploma back to his old school in Tabora where he filled the post as a teacher of biology.

In 1949 Julius Nyerere won a scholarship to Edinburgh University, the first Tanganyikan to attend a British university. As he studied for a master's degree, Julius was already fired with a determination to build his country into a proud, self-reliant nation. To help toward his keep, he sorted mail in a local post office.

Back home again, Julius Nyerere taught biology at the Saint Francis School at Pugu near Dar es Salaam. It was there he saw the Tanganyika African Association, TAA, as the instrument through which he could work for Tanganyika's independence.

TAA was a social club at that time but, as the club's president, Nyerere changed the name to the Tanganyika African National Union, TANU, and drafted a new constitution that transformed it into a political machine. He called upon TANU members to

President Nyerere swears in John Malecela as the first minister for foreign affairs.

work for independence, to consistently oppose racial discrimination, to resist tribalism, and to fight for local and national elections that could gain African majorities. Nyerere stressed that freedom would come, not by violence, but with the support of a strengthened TANU.

In the meantime Nyerere had married Maria Gabriel, a tall, graceful girl from a northern district. But in a drive for increased

TANU membership he left his bride and toured the country in a dilapidated Land Rover, stopping to speak before thousands of village meetings.

Nyerere had adopted a sort of uniform—a green bush shirt and slacks—but it was his lively humor and shining, intelligent countenance that won for TANU the support of every group he addressed. Nyerere made it clear to every audience that he preferred the title "Mwalimu" as a reminder of his former occupation, and that he wished to maintain the same relationship with the people. *Mwalimu* in the Swahili language means "teacher."

Back in the party's headquarters in Dar es Salaam, Nyerere and his colleagues were suffering the extremes of poverty for they had resigned their various occupations in order to give full time to boosting the cause of TANU. Maria Nyerere opened a small shop, a *duka,* and also took in sewing to help make ends meet.

Nyerere saw the value of the feminine voice in the cause and a partition now divided the crowded mud-walled TANU headquarters to accommodate the new women's branch. He enlisted the aid of Bibi Titi Mohammed, a plump, eloquent grandmother of the Muslim faith, who defied Muslim laws with her successful public campaigning.

Inspired by Bibi's forcefulness women organized the United Women of Tanganyika, UWT, with Bibi as the first president. "We are determined to help . . . against poverty, ignorance, and disease. . . ." she shouted to one receptive audience.

Women formed committees and sponsored fund-raising projects. Maria Nyerere was put in charge of UWT's poultry-raising farm. Groups of UWT members raised corn and rice on one twenty-acre farm, and thirteen thousand coconut trees and 203 head of cattle on another. The women's liberation movement in action was a force that demanded respect and to many outsiders UWT members deserved all the credit for bringing TANU to power.

TANU flourished. Their numbers had increased from twenty branches in 1955 with one hundred thousand members, to forty-eight branches in 1957 with two hundred thousand members. By 1959 there were one million paid TANU members, and ten years later an additional half million.

Maria Nyerere (*left*) was among the Tanzanian women who welcomed Mrs. Milton Obote (in white) when she arrived in Dar es Salaam with her husband, then president of Uganda, for a conference.

Under Nyerere's direction, TANU had emerged as a vigorous political party by 1955 with a nation-conscious people solidly behind its aim for independence. TANU members saw that it was time for their leader to fly to the United Nations in New York.

Julius Nyerere set a precedent by being the first political leader from East Africa to speak before the United Nations. With his talent for words, Nyerere presented his argument "against a colonial system which qualified the rights of an individual according to the color of his skin." He spoke without rancor, an attitude that pleased a listening world.

A women's contingent of People's Militia.

In 1956, Nyerere appeared again before the United Nations, calling for universal adult suffrage and a definite timetable for Tanganyika's constitutional advancement.

Though impatient for independence, even Nyerere was surprised at the swiftness with which independence came. He had spoken to his people saying, "By hard work, either in our own lifetime or that of our children, we shall achieve it," yet three years later, the first general election was held. Parliament had passed a law that established the right to vote with a requirement that every voter must vote for a candidate for each of the three races—African, Asian, and European. TANU received an overwhelming majority of the African votes and most Asian and European as well.

In 1960, Nyerere was made chief minister when TANU won seventy of seventy-one elected seats in a second general election under British supervision, but for the establishment of self-rule.

Britain granted internal self-government in May of 1961, and later in the year, full independence with Julius K. Nyerere as prime minister. In his independence message Nyerere included these words:

We have agreed that our nation shall be a nation of free and equal citizens, each person having an equal right and opportunity to develop himself and contribute to the maximum of his capabilities to the development of our society . . . yet . . . poverty, ignorance, and disease must be overcome before we can really establish in this country the sort of society we have been dreaming of . . . . From now on we are fighting not man but nature and we are seeking to wrest from na-

Mr. Julius Nyerere (*left*) smilingly steps out of office on January 22, 1961, as Mr. Rashidi Kawawa becomes the new prime minister.

ture a better and fuller life for ourselves. In this struggle the only weapon is our determination and our own effort.

The awareness of the urgency to "wrest from nature a better life" obliged Nyerere to resign the prime ministership one month later. Mr. Rashidi Kawawa replaced him.

Rashidi Kawawa was born in 1930, the son of a government employee. As a young man he worked for movie companies, quickly advancing to the position of film supervisor. At the same time he became a star movie actor. But Rashidi Kawawa's interests leaned strongly toward the rights of workers and community development. He renounced his movie career for politics and was the first person to organize workers' committees—or unions. In 1956 he was asked to head them. Rashidi Kawawa joined the central government in 1960 and soon proved to be a staunch ally in the fight for freedom.

Confident that the country's leadership was in capable hands Mwalimu Nyerere took to the field in his Land Rover. He toured the country north, west, and south, as he spurred the jubilant masses into accepting his new slogan—no longer Uhuru, but *Uhuru na Kozi*—"Freedom and Work."

In November of 1962, Nyerere was elected president. A month later the new nation, still known as Tanganyika, became a republic within the British Commonwealth of Nations, a group of independent countries sharing somewhat similar historical backgrounds.

President Nyerere admires buffaloes presented by the United Arab Republic on a visit to Cairo.

4

The Island of Cloves

The island of Zanzibar in the Indian Ocean lies within twenty miles of the Tanzanian coast. Its history and that of the mainland are interwoven over many centuries. Intrepid explorers made Zanzibar their headquarters before setting off for Africa's unknown interior. And it was to Zanzibar that captured African slaves were shipped from the coastal port of Bagamoyo. Though between thirty thousand and forty thousand slaves were sold at auction each year, this is less than half the number of captives to survive the long march down to the Arab dhows that waited to transport them to Zanzibar's auction blocks.

On the night of January 12, 1964, Mwalimu Nyerere's attention was diverted from campaigning for the good of his people. From Zanzibar news of revolution reached the mainland. Within one month of Zanzibar's achieving independence the island's Afro-Shirazi party, acting through the Revolutionary Council, had overthrown the Arab minority government. The melee left five hundred slaughtered Arabs and widespread property destruction.

The revolt was hardly unexpected. The beautiful islands of

Zanzibar and less-populated Pemba have a long history of exploitation by Sunnite Arabs of the indigenous Shirazi and mainland Africans. Of a total population of about 300,000, the Shirazi number 230,000, but the Arabs were the masters, having assumed control of East Africa during the eighteenth century. Rumbles of discontent among the Shirazi had erupted repeatedly but they had to curb their impatience, not yet having attained the educational and economic resources of the Arab minority. But their impatience quickened as each new African nation emerged and the independence movement swept Africa.

The original Shirazi people emigrated to Zanzibar from the Persian city of Shiraz some time during the twelfth century. They found a community of Sunnites already established on the islands. Although both groups observed the Islamic religion, tensions between the two groups developed immediately, for the Sunnites were orthodox Muslims and the Shirazi were unorthodox. When in 1828 a further influx of Sunnites included the Imam of Oman, Sayyid Said, the ill feeling was intensified.

The sultan made the islands his capital and at once started to develop them commercially, mainly with large plantations of cloves, the aromatic dried flower buds of a tropical tree, and copra—dried coconut meat. It was on the plantations that he used forced Shirazi and African labor.

The abominable though lucrative slave trade was active until 1848 when the British partially stopped it. But the practice continued on the two islands' plantations, though to a lesser degree.

A weakened sultan turned to Britain for help and in 1890 the islands became British protectorates. Then, in 1897, the British Anti-Slavery Society succeeded in bringing about a complete cessation of the slave trade. Arab power in East Africa ended except in Zanzibar where the sultan received annual stipends from the landowners that enabled him to live with a show of pomp.

The Afro-Shirazi party was always strongly supported by TANU. It was formed in 1957 when two different parties combined to fight the elections of that year. Though the party won a majority of seats in that and subsequent elections, its leaders were denied any authority in government.

After a general election in June, 1963, the contesting Arab-dominated Nationalist party decided to join with the Zanzibar and Pemba People's party, ZPPP. Although the Afro-Shirazi party had gained the largest number of seats and more than half the total votes, the Nationalist-ZPPP coalition continued to retain power and form the government after independence.

No wonder, then, that the people of Zanzibar rose in anger and ousted the sultan and his government, replacing him with Sheikh Abeid A. Karume, the leader of the Afro-Shirazi party.

For a time chaos prevailed in Zanzibar. Thousands of Arabs were deported. Asians were terrorized, most British government employees were dismissed, and a team of Americans who manned a space-tracking station was evicted.

When the Revolutionary Council invited Chinese, East German, Russian, and Yugoslav missions to the island an alarmed Western World anxiously focused its attention on every Zanzibari move.

For East Germany, this was the first success in establishing an embassy in a non-Communist country. They responded magnificently with offers to improve housing, supply technical advisors, build a radio transmitter for propaganda programs in Swahili, and to supply a fleet of fishing boats. The Chinese sent a shipload of buses, and the Russians volunteered to reorganize Zanzibar's harbor system.

Then Mwalimu Nyerere paid a visit to President Karume. Following a prolonged conference, an announcement was issued. Tanganyika and Zanzibar had decided to join. By using the first

Minister of Communications, Works, and Labor, Mr. J. Lusinde (*third from left*), walks through dense bush with Chinese railway survey team in Ulanga.

syllables of the names of their respective countries they would be the United Republic of Tanzania. The memorable date was April 23, 1964.

Julius K. Nyerere was named president of the new republic, Abeid A. Karume the first vice-president, and Rashidi Kawawa

Tanzanian dancers greet President Sékou Touré of Guinea on a state visit. On the left is Second Vice-President Rashidi Kawawa.

the second vice-president. A new cabinet was formed in Dar es Salaam which included most of the original ministers with the addition of six Zanzibaris. That all embassies on Zanzibar would be reduced to consular status was a sad disappointment to the East Germans.

A new constitution lay down the power to each of the two governments—the Union government and the Zanzibar government. But by agreement between the two governments, duties previously assumed by the Zanzibar government gradually came to be the responsibility of the Union government.

An appropriate coat-of-arms was designed for the new republic. The shield, upheld by the figures of a man and a woman, is rich in symbolism. A flame at the top of the shield signifies freedom and knowledge and a yellow background represents the mineral wealth of the countries. The Tanzanian flag is under the flame—a black and yellow diagonal stripe with green at the top left and blue at the bottom right. A vertical spear for defense and a crossed axe and hoe, as the tools of the people, are centered. The human figures stand on a representation of Mount Kilimanjaro. Each figure holds an elephant tusk, symbolizing the abundant wildlife. At the man's feet is a clove tree, representing a major product of Zanzibar. At the woman's feet a cotton plant represents a major product of Tanganyika. But the slogan on the scroll that spreads across the base carries the full meaning of the handsome coat-of-arms. It reads *Uhuru na Umoja*—"Freedom and Unity." It is a fitting emblem for the voluntary coming together of two equal nations.

The union is important to mainland Tanzania. The island would act as a bulwark against surprise attacks from countries not yet governed by African people, such as Mozambique to the immediate south, and the Republic of South Africa. Extreme caution is exercised in allowing any strangers from these countries and Rhodesia to enter Tanzania in case they are spies. However, mainland Tanzania is a refuge for anyone officially connected with liberation movements such as FRELIMO in Mozambique whose members work for freedom from Portugal, the African National Congress in South Africa (ANC), the Southwest People's Organization (SWAPO), and the Zimbabwe African National Union in Rhodesia (ZANU). The Tanzanian government maintains headquarters for each of the four organizations, schools for refugee children, and training camps for guerrilla movements.

Though the Union has grown stronger through the years since 1964, at times relations between Zanzibar and Tanzania have been strained. Unlike President Nyerere whose mild socialist tendencies have produced a response of loyalty and trust in the people, Vice-President Karume's authoritarian and iron-fisted policies had aroused a smoldering antagonism. On the evening of April 8, 1972, Karume was attacked by four assassins at the political headquarters. He was killed and two members of his Revolutionary Council were wounded. However, the assassination was not followed by any attempt to overthrow the government. Aboud Jumbe, formerly a minister of state in the first vice-president's office, replaced Abeid Karume as vice-president of the United Republic of Tanzania.

5

The President and Foreign Aid

President Nyerere and his TANU party were aware that building a nation was a greater challenge than winning independence, and that exacting organization was necessary. In July, 1964, the United Republic Parliament approved Tanzania's first Five-Year Plan. Primarily, the plan was designed for the benefit and welfare of the people by having government enter directly into the management of goods and services. It would improve living conditions for the farmers, provide education for all children, and protect the health of families. The plan contained measures that were intended to transform Tanzania into a socialist country.

A formidable task lay ahead and foreign aid, in the form of investment, government grants, and loans, was necessary before such an ambitious program could be realized.

The response to Tanzania's needs was immediate and gratifying. Britain, Israel, West Germany, and the United States were so infected by Tanzanian enthusiasm for building a real nation that they, among other nations, lent some millions of dollars toward development. Foreign engineers, teachers, and technicians sped to Tanzania to advise on special construction and industrial projects. Organizations such as UNICEF and the International Red Cross helped in times of drought and flood.

At the opening ceremony of the Hale hydroelectric scheme near Tanga, Mwalimu Nyerere expressed his country's gratitude for one British gesture, saying "I said that when we became independent, in ten years we would do more for the development of this country than the British did in their forty years here. . . . The British could have said, 'Very well, we shall stay away for ten years . . . then we shall see if you have fulfilled your promise. . . .' Instead they have said, 'We will send you technicians to help. . . . We will also give you loans and grants to help you show that you can do in ten years what we failed to do in forty.' Nothing could be more generous. . . ."

Care was taken by the Union government to keep to a policy of nonalignment and not all offers of help were accepted when conditions were attached that would affect national independence. Nyerere strictly observed the policy of nonalignment in keeping a balance between Asian and Western bounty. He sent a delegation to Peking, led by Mr. Kawawa, that received the promise of a $45-million interest-free loan. The delegates were no sooner back in Dar es Salaam than a Chinese freighter docked and unloaded automatic weapons, rifles, and eleven experts to train Tanzanians in their use.

At a public presentation of the munificent gift, the Chinese ambassador in Dar es Salaam promised that his country would build the largest textile mill in East Africa, also a five-thousand-acre state farm and farm implement factory.

A protest came from Washington concerning Tanzania's involvement with Red China, but Mwalimu Nyerere replied that

President Nyerere unveils a plaque to officially open the Chinese-built Tanzanian People's Defense Force naval base at Kigamboni near Dar es Salaam.

Tanzania had already welcomed scores of technicians and 350 Peace Corps workers from America. He also quelled China's hopes for a closer relationship by stating that ". . . neither our

principles nor our freedom to determine our own future is for
sale."

Rashidi Kawawa led successful economic missions to Russia,
Poland, Czechoslovakia, and West Germany. Prominent in aid
was West Germany's gift of $150,000 for a two-hundred-bed hos-
pital to be built near Mount Kilimanjaro and prompt help in organizing an air force; and from Canada in organizing the United
Republic army.

When Mr. Abdulrahma Babu, one Zanzibari cabinet minister,
voiced an opinion that "Trade, not aid, is Tanzania's best hope
for the future," investors showed their confidence in Tanzania's
nation-building projects by installing oil refineries and textile
factories. Manufacturing rope from the three hundred thousand
tons of sisal that were harvested each year, and making matches
and their boxes from timber cut from Kilimanjaro's forests were
among new industries that were set up.

Considering that Tanzania's policies for progress were designed for the benefit and welfare of the people, accepting foreign
loans, grants, investments, ultimately meant the building of better lives for all Tanzanians—the peasant farmers, the owners of
the land. But Mwalimu Nyerere declared, after returning from
one of his month-long inspection tours of villages, that the peasant farmer did not fully understand, or practice, *Uhuru na Kozi*.
Again, there was an urgent need for government reorganization.

On February 5, of 1967, and under the direction of TANU,
the Arusha Declaration was made public at an important meeting in Arusha. The Declaration contained clauses that for a
while dampened the hopes of foreign investors.

6

The Arusha Declaration

When TANU leaders met in Arusha they based the country's new policies on the TANU creed with its principles of socialism which believes that all people are equal, and every citizen is an integral part of the nation, and has the right to receive from society protection of his life and property and a just reward for his labors.

Socialism as an ideology is only effective when people strongly believe in its principles and are prepared to practice them. The first duty of a TANU member is to live by these principles. In particular he should never live by another's labor, nor should he have capitalist or feudalist tendencies. No TANU or government leader should hold shares in any business or directorships in any privately owned enterprises. He should never receive two or more salaries, own more than one car, or own houses which he rents to others.

The president had already reduced his own salary by 20 percent when in October of 1965 he was reelected by a 96.5 percent approval vote on both the mainland and Zanzibar. Now the gesture was adopted by other TANU and government officials as part of the proscribed austerity program.

In presenting the Arusha Declaration, Mwalimu Nyerere outlined the course for a socialist society based on rural development, self-reliance, and the labor of the masses that own the country—therefore the products of the land. Rather than lose the benefits from the fruits of the land, and thus their independence, the government planned to take over the businesses that had direct influences on the basic needs of the people.

The Declaration was presented in three sectors—one consisting of wholly-owned government enterprises, another with government-controlled enterprises, and a third with a few enterprises open to private investment. It was the pronouncement that foreign-owned banks, insurance companies, import-export firms, and some factories were to be nationalized, that discouraged new overseas investors who for a time withheld their support.

In part, these are words spoken by Mwalimu Nyerere in his summing up of the Declaration: "We talk about money and our search for money increases our efforts, but it would be more appropriate . . . to spend time in the villages showing the people how to bring about development through their own efforts. From now on we shall know what is the foundation and what is the fruit of development. Between money and people it is obvious that the people and their hard work are the foundation of development and money is one of the fruits of that work.

"From now on we shall stand upright and walk forward on our feet rather than look at this problem upside down. Industries will come and money will come but their foundation is the people and their hard work, especially in *agriculture*. This is the meaning of self-reliance. . . ."

TANU members then expressed their enthusiasm by leading long marches through the country, explaining the purpose of the Declaration as they progressed. One epic march was led by Mwalimu Nyerere, from his home town of Butami to Mwanza, a distance of 138 miles. The march took eight days to complete. It

A view of the Azimio monument in Arusha with members of the public awaiting its inauguration by President Nyerere.

grew in numbers, for the president's eloquent speaking gained hundreds of supporters along the route.

Material proof was already apparent by the end of 1967 that the system worked, and so restored the confidence of foreign investors who took advantage of the long-term benefits of building Tanzania's economy on a sound political basis. Among the contributors was the United States which allotted some $16.5 million as aid in reconstructing a road that leads into Zambia.

Non-African Tanzanian residents who were most affected by the Arusha Declaration were the Indians—or Asians. Though numbering only eighty thousand approximately, they were in command of Tanzania's commerce, both retail and wholesale. Now their businesses were to be controlled by government, their work permits were unrenewable, and with no choice in the matter they were obliged to leave the country. On Zanzibar as recently as October, 1971, some three hundred Asian traders were stripped of their licenses. Though most of them and their twelve hundred dependents had been born on the island, they were threatened with deportation.

The new system was under the direction of TANU and operated by the National Development Corporation, NDC, that officially came into existence in December, 1964, "to facilitate and promote the economic development of Tanzania."

After the Arusha Declaration the National Assembly passed the Industrial Shares Act, naming seven companies in which NDC was to acquire a majority shareholding. As NDC grew, its headquarters moved to a new and larger head office in Dar es Salaam where it was reorganized into six departments, the National Agricultural and Food Corporation, NAFCO, being of prime importance.

NDC's portfolio of investments expanded at a prodigious rate. Its officers were constantly busy incorporating, taking over or closing companies, and transferring or acquiring shares in more than fifty-seven companies comprising wide interest—from bicycles to auto tires. But more than half the shares of a company whose business pertained to the products of the land, such as cashew nuts, were held by local villages and cooperative societies.

Socialist system benefits came quickly for the man on the land.

7

Ujamaa Villages

Ujamaa means "familyhood" in the Swahili language and *viji-jini* means "village." In most parts of Africa the practice of families living together in villages on a communal basis is common, but a "ujamaa village" has a different connotation under the present successful system.

The small farmer who lives in a rural area subsists on very little income—as low an average as eighty-five dollars annually. And since 90 percent of Tanzania's people work as farmers it is important that the development program should pay close consideration to the farmer and his needs. It is expected, and obligatory if the plan is to be worthy of the effort, that farmers raise the quality of their crops and increase the yield by at least 7 percent before they can expect the better things of life. The resulting success, or failure, of the scheme depends entirely on the efforts of the man with the hoe and on all the people working together as a ujamaa village with a single purpose—that of producing more and better crops.

In the first days of independence TANU encouraged farming families to group together in rural areas. The government pro-

vided all sorts of modern equipment such as fertilizers, to improve the soil, and tractors for harvesting the crops. It installed
social services and it initiated schemes that demanded the closest
cooperation of the people involved.

But, though the people on the land welcomed Mwalimu Nyerere's and TANU leaders' periodic visits with great enthusiasm,
the productiveness of their lands did not increase one whit. In
many cases the heavy capital investment was wasted. Tanzania's
president once said, "While some nations are trying to reach the
moon, we are trying to reach the village." He pondered the problem, then looked for a remedy.

During the year 1968, Mwalimu Nyerere made a statement

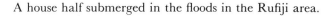

A house half submerged in the floods in the Rufiji area.

concerning past wrongs committed in rural development. "We were thinking in terms of *things*, not *people*," he said, "that capital investment would lead to increased output . . . to a transformation in the lives of the people involved. The people were secondary; the first priority was the output. The ujamaa village is a new conception, based on the understanding that what we need to develop is *people*, not *things*, and that people can only develop themselves."

Since that time, self-reliance has been the approach to rural development which operates under a system called Community Development, CD. Ujamaa villages are owned and governed by those who live and work in them. A government official can advise but may not tell villagers what they can do, or plant, or how they must divide the labor, though every village member (except the very young, the old, and the crippled) must work. They alone decide how to use the money they earn jointly.

TANU trains teams of workers at Tengoru College as advisors to ujamaa villages. The college, situated near Arusha, accommodates 128 young men at a time who receive a six-month course in CD principles, followed by six months' practical experience in fieldwork. The recruits have a further four months' training at the school before they qualify as CD assistants. There are also two CD home economics training centers for women, and available CD courses in small businesses, in trade, basic health, and local government.

To create a ujamaa village, each CD worker's role includes some use of psychology, for he first increases the villagers' dissatisfaction with the meagerness of their lives. He draws attention to certain conveniences they lack—perhaps a village needs running water or electricity—then he helps them find ways of earning the money to obtain the comforts that will bring pleasure into their lives. The CD official suggests means of raising a village's economic level, but he refrains from making decisions. The villagers decide among themselves the methods they will use to raise their standard of living, a philosophy that is in line with African tradition where every question is debated within the group.

A new ujamaa village is never left completely to its own devices. It receives assistance from the government when a project cannot be completed by self-reliance alone. For instance, the villagers may have dug a new and deeper well. They have used

Coffee of fine quality is grown in Northern Province.

Pyrethrum is gathered in Southern Highlands.

what money the village has saved to buy the pipes and to install them, but they have no money left for buying the pump. Then CD provides the pump.

Sometimes CD moves farming families from less productive areas to form settlements of one hundred or more villages, supporting approximately sixty-five thousand people. Some farmers are at first unwilling to move to a new site if it means leaving their cattle behind them. But group ujamaas foster the spirit of cooperation as each farmer works his own one acre of land in addition to communal holdings. One successful venture is recorded that shows a yield of fifteen hundred pounds of cotton an acre as compared to an average individual's four hundred pounds an acre. The farmers built a dam with the proceeds from the sale of their bales of cotton through a local cooperative.

One ambitious CD undertaking started in 1970 when it established ujamaa villages for 750,000 residents from the vicinity of Dodoma, one of Tanzania's poorest regions. An official of the Ministry of Lands, Housing, and Urban Development arrived in the region, bringing with him seventy-two surveyors in eighteen teams who at once started outlining and placing the villages.

These settlements are called blocks and have a developing officer and a staff of specialists as consultants. Each block supports a service center, clinic, market, school, DC and cooperative offices, a playing field, and a police station. Several blocks are grouped into districts which are under the supervision of a state Development Commission.

A group of students from the Kivukoni Training College for development workers in Dar es Salaam visited a ujamaa village near Tanga. Their report serves as a good example of coordination at work. The village is located in sisal-growing country. Though the growing and processing of sisal is the main occupation, the condition of the soil and the climate are suitable for growing a variety of foods. The farmers have four hundred acres under sisal and two hundred acres under corn, but these ambitious people intend to eventually cultivate four thousand acres.

The day begins with a whistle call at 6:00 A.M. The workers assemble outside the village office and receive their orders which are distributed by the farm manager. The amount of work expected of each person is fixed. For sisal harvesting, using only ex-

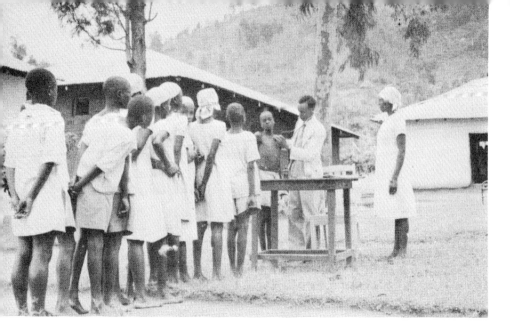

Periodic checkups by visiting doctors carry the fight against disease even into remote mountain villages.

perienced cutters, the standard is fifty bunches of thirty leaves each per day. The women's job is to beat the corn grains from the cobs, each woman being required to fill three four-gallon tins in a day.

Village leaders hold discussions in the evenings. And as good leaders they remember that their responsible positions are ones of trust and that they are the servants of the people rather than the masters. This attitude induces a harmonious atmosphere that makes members feel free to discuss the affairs of their ujamaa, including profitable means of investing their capital which is lodged in a cooperative savings bank.

Already these villagers have financed one woman's training at a nursing school. A new dispensary in the village will be ready when she has completed her course. They have sent away one youth for training in animal husbandry, and another young man for truck-driving lessons. The villagers will have a driver but must still rent a truck from a cooperative for carrying their large harvest of sisal to the processing center. They debated whether they should seek a loan from the Region Development Fund for buying their own truck.

The students from Kivukoni College brought up for discussion the practice of burning weeds and dead plants rather than collecting and using them as green manure. After debating the advisability of such an innovation, the villagers gave the students one acre of land to prove by demonstration that the theory would work.

Perhaps CD workers consider their greatest achievement was drawing the Masai tribes into the plan. As cattle herders only, the dignified Masai traditionally spurned any form of manual labor except to throw together in a haphazard manner their temporary dome-shaped homes of mud. It was an unprecedented event when CD officials persuaded twenty Masai warriors to operate a six-hundred-acre farm and to build a bridge at a strategic point across one river. Never before had a Masai used a hoe, or a cement-mixer, or had broken stones and toted them, but they, too, became infected with the spirit of nation-building. The Masai leader pledged his support of the Development Plan. Masai cattle were a serious threat to Tanzania's economy, having taken over one-third of all arable land, but the pledge included reducing the number of their cattle and increasing the quality for feeding Tanzania's people and for export through one or more of the 150 cattle cooperatives.

The cooperative movement plays an important role in Tanzania's economic future. The coffee-growing Chagga tribes in Moshi organized the first cooperative which sold their coffee at higher prices on the London market. With the profits, the Chagga people built an imposing headquarters and several schools. Other centers like Mwanza on Lake Victoria, followed with a cotton cooperative. The tobacco industry in the southern town of Songea organized cooperatives, followed by the fishing and dairy industries. Livestock, rice, and cashew nuts, even gold and diamond mines have cooperatives. And in Dar es Salaam there is a co-op taxi fleet.

Today, all produce except tea and sisal is marketed through cooperative societies under the control of government commodity boards.

Not only are cooperatives the links between producer and consumer, but their presence keeps the farmers in ujamaa villages cognizant that from co-ops come the tangible rewards for their hard work. Co-ops act as incentives to grow fatter cattle and sweeter corn. They are the reminders that the people of Tanzania are the owners of the land which, through individual effort, will grow ever more productive under the president's TANU Development Plan.

8

The War Against Ignorance

Tanzanians eagerly accepted a plan set up by Rashidi Ka-wawa for remedying the country's shockingly high illiteracy rate. He introduced this vital function as the "People's Education Plan." At the time of independence 80 percent of the men and 89 percent of the women could not read or write, and such a plan looked to the future as an important preparation for Tanzania's place in the world of nations.

Inadequate facilities for schoolchildren accommodated only half of their number of which 75 percent dropped out before reaching high school. A mere one percent attended college. This condition also needed remedying.

But the plan aimed at educating adults first by having CD workers induce ujamaa leaders to start adult classes. Discussions centered on local and national affairs in addition to instruction in English and Swahili and general knowledge. The Tanzania Broadcasting Company cooperated by beaming courses in both languages on grade and high school levels. Sometimes the station staff members would dramatize the lessons which TBC accompanied with appropriate background sound effects.

Not all adult classes took place in ujamaas Training centers in each of fifty-seven districts offered brief courses in agriculture, trade, and good health. Once a week, because there was a critical shortage, the TBC broadcast a program for incipient teachers.

The government placed classes within the reach of every Tanzanian citizen. They were even available for prison inmates who were given certificates upon completion of the course. Builders, merchants, and varied artisans attended literacy classes to learn elementary arithmetic and geometry for use in their trades. But in most classes women were in the majority, and classes in sewing and cooking were exclusively theirs.

The Kivukoni College was organized soon after independence with thirty-nine students, selected mainly from among TANU and government cooperative staffs. TANU raised $30,000 for the project, the government $20,000, and West Germany $25,000.

One active group of young people in Tanzania is the TANU Youth League whose members volunteer their services in a number of projects and in emergencies such as floods and epidemics. As teachers of adult classes they excel. Bibi Titi Mohammed, prior to her responsible job as leader of the Women's Movement, mastered her English in a TYL classroom. Her enthusiasm drove her to launch a campaign urging graduate high school girls to volunteer for literacy teaching and self-help projects.

But by far the most popular classes were those given for learning to read and write Swahili which, with English, is Tanzania's official language. In a Swahili class each student is given a notebook, an eraser-tipped pencil, and a textbook titled *Jifunze Kusoma*, which means "Learn to Read." The book presents important social and economic content through the stories of Bwana Matata (trouble) and Bwana Chapakazi (hardworker) and their families while teaching the basic skills of reading and writing. Later books continue to help adults become functional literates, useful to their society.

The enthusiasm for education filtered through to younger children who made full use of "self-help in the home" grade schools that TANU had started in the early days of independence. They were sponsored by the Tanganyikan African Parents' Association and by 1964 had grown to number twenty-five hundred small schools with one hundred thousand students.

Schools were mainly in the hands of missionary societies prior to independence. They were subsidized by the colonial govern-

Kindergarten class learning to write.

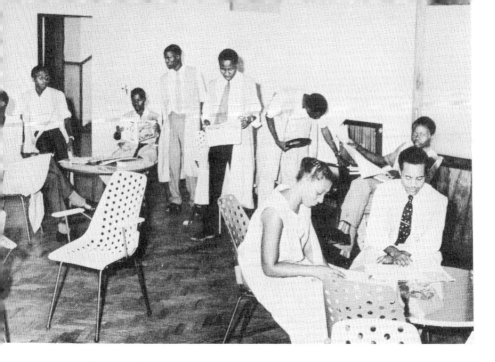

Law students take time out for relaxation at University College, Dar es Salaam.

ment which trained teachers for employment in their own schools and those provided by every big European farm and place of business. And though missionaries were dedicated, conscientious persons, their chief function was proselytizing. Moreover, the system was British and not designed to prepare children for their country's service, but rather to instill in them the value of a colonial society.

After independence, missions still provided the education for 250,000 students in about three thousand schools. But only 480 students had advanced to high school. There were no facilities for university-level education at all, and until TANU founded the University College in Dar es Salaam in October, 1961, students sought higher education elsewhere. In 1960 there were 215 Tanganyikan students enrolled in the Makerere University College in Uganda, 27 in the Royal Technical College in Kenya, and 77 overseas.

Mwalimu Nyerere was far from satisfied with Tanzania's system of education as a whole. In a paper he wrote during 1967, he pointed out that grade school was nothing but a preparation for high school and though children aspired to further education, 87 percent were denied the opportunity because of the lack of facilities. The process was repeated when entrance to a college or university was the issue. In his words, "The system now provided is designed for the few who are intellectually stronger . . . it induces . . . a feeling of superiority, and leaves the majority of the others hankering after something they will never attain. . . . It induces the growth of a class structure." Mwalimu Nyerere saw the need for educational integration with Tanzania's national life.

Tanzania, with an abundance of land but very little capital, will have a rural economy for a long time. But the educational system still needs revision. Students have to journey many miles to attend high school. They live in dormitories, eat well, and are not required to perform any manual work. They get used to having their food prepared by servants, their dishes washed, and their rooms cleaned. The situation is even more accentuated for college students. So the gulf widens between the student and his farming family which he visits, reluctantly, during vacation periods. He does not offer help on the farm because he is afraid of soiling his hands. And his proud parents do not expect him to help. They see their offspring as one of the elite who will one day sit in a fine office and draw a large salary.

Mwalimu Nyerere wrote that ". . . Our pupils learn to despise even their own parents because they are old-fashioned and ignorant . . . and nothing in our existing system suggests to the pupil that he can learn things about farming from his elders."

President Nyerere then announced a major change in emphasis in Tanzanian education. Agriculture would be taught along with academic subjects, and schools would produce their own foodstuffs. Children would begin grade school at an older age and be prepared to return to farming upon completion of primary education. They would learn by doing, which is merely a return to the traditional method of education.

TANU opened the University College as a law school with an enrollment of fourteen students. By 1969, the college had already enrolled more than 400 students and produced 300 graduates. By 1964 it had established a faculty of arts with 94 students. By 1969 the number had risen to 935 with most graduates becoming high school teachers. Faculties of science, medicine, and agriculture came later and each has grown in proportion.

Several institutes are affiliated to the University College; among them are the Institute of Adult Education which trains teachers of adults, and the Institute of Swahili Research which aims to preserve and develop the Swahili language.

On July 1, 1970, the University College became the University of Dar es Salaam—Tanzania's first university. Now fully equipped and financed by the people of Tanzania, the well-planned buildings, set in a beautiful campus on Observation Hill, anticipate having a student body that increases through the years. From an expected 673 graduates in 1974, it is likely to be producing more than one thousand graduates by the late 1970's.

Along with his blessings at his installation as chancellor, President Nyerere added, "We expect that our university will be of such a nature that all who pass through it will be prepared both in knowledge and in attitude for giving maximum service to the community."

President Nyerere remembers an earlier recommendation that "The education provided by Tanzania for the students of Tanzania must serve the purpose of Tanzania. It must encourage the development of a proud, independent, and free citizenry which relies upon itself for its own development, and which knows the advantages and the problems of cooperation. . . . Let the students be educated to be members and servants of the kind of just and egalitarian future to which this country aspires."

9

Prevention and Cure

In 1968 the first six qualified doctors graduated from the faculty of medicine of the University College. At the time, forty-five Tanzanians were in practice along with some 400 foreign doctors who were either employed by the government or industrial firms, in private practice, or engaged in research. The missions provided the services of 110 doctors on the list. But even with the assistance of an army of medical aides, nurses, midwives, and health inspectors, their total was hardly adequate for handling Tanzania's high rate of ill health.

Tanzania is afflicted with most of the world's communicable diseases which, with malnutrition, account for a short life span. It is sad indeed that almost half of Tanzania's children fail to reach adulthood. But by concentration on prevention and education, by 1980 the government expects to have raised the average life expectancy from thirty-five years to fifty years. The expense of seeing this ambitious plan through to satisfactory fulfillment will be borne by the government, local authorities, and voluntary services such as missions.

The missionaries were the first to bring a knowledge of modern medicine to Tanzania. Their supplies were limited but they diligently attacked the scourges of malaria, smallpox, cholera, and other endemic diseases. And as long ago as 1888, missionaries recognized that one of their Tanzanian assistants possessed a remarkable talent for healing. They sent him away to Malta to study. When he returned the missionaries set him up in his own small hospital in Karema. Even Dr. David Livingstone, the doctor-explorer, found time from waging his war against the slave traffic to open a clinic beside the well-trodden route from the coast to Lake Tanganyika.

When from 1886 to 1919 the Germans occupied Tanzania as a colony called German East Africa, they launched the first mass vaccination campaign against smallpox. And the British, during their occupation of Tanzania, concentrated on eliminating yaws, a contagious skin disease. Though unable to entirely wipe out the malaria-bearing mosquito by spraying with residual insecticides, by using improved drugs the British succeeded in lessening the virulence of malaria.

In the early days, village medicine men looked upon foreign doctors as their chief rivals and antagonists. And the distrust of the one for the other was mutual. A medicine man's belief that all sickness stemmed from an offense against an ancestor spirit was anathema to European doctors. And the harsh treatment a medicine man administered so filled a patient with fear that many times he was made even sicker. Today, a medicine man's influence is more in the role of psychologist who advises in times of distress. It has been found upon analysis, however, that some herbal medicines he prescribes include ingredients that today's African scientists include in their medications. Mothers still derive comfort from having their babies and young children wear strings of white beads around their necks, wrists, and ankles, for medicine men declare that the wearing of white beads will ward off evil spirits.

People who live in rural areas have been educated against sometimes harmful superstitions through the use of posters and what they hear in hygiene and homemaking classes.

Since the belief in the powers of medicine men has decreased, Tanzania's people have turned more and more to services offered by medical centers. Health education and a resulting rise in population also have a great deal to do with the demands upon Tanzania's sorely overtaxed facilities.

The government has commenced a health program that places the emphasis on prevention. The plan is divided into four categories—better nutrition, better water supply, better care for mothers and children, and the control of communicable diseases.

Poor nutrition is the number one cause of Tanzania's high infant mortality. As soon as they are weaned, little children eat a sort of cornmeal mush made from corn their mothers grind in huge mortars, and not much else. Traveling teams from the Ministry of Health now advise villagers that corn, though a substantial food, does not supply the vitamins and proteins that are necessary for good health. Representatives from the Ministry of Agriculture induce villagers to grow green vegetables and fruits. They advise children to "Drink more milk." In orchard country, growers now transport canned orange juice throughout the country. And cattlemen distribute beef to fill the protein needs. Experts on wildlife periodically thin the herds of antelope which Tanzania has in abundance, then sell the venison in cooperative markets. The United Nations Children's Fund, UNICEF, the United Nations Food and Agricultural Organization, and several

Dental clinic in Dar es Salaam.

Student nurses receive practical demonstration.

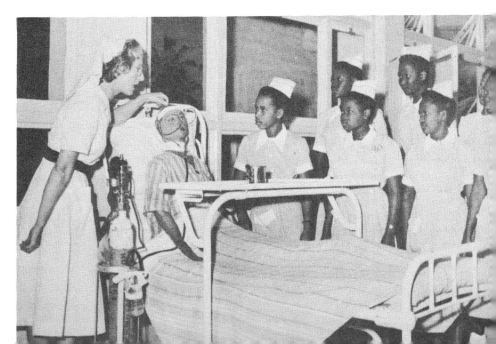

private organizations give valuable support to the vital need to improve nutrition and ease Tanzania's health problems.

Water is a carrier of a variety of diseases and a more consistent and cleaner water supply is being piped to rural areas. Health inspectors demonstrate the necessity of boiling drinking water, and the need for improved sanitation. During one hookworm epidemic, members of TANU's Youth League aided medical officers by persuading people to build improved outhouses. Within four months of the start of their campaign, four thousand homes had new toilets.

Contaminated water is the source of one enervating disease called bilharzia—microscopic parasites which lurk in snails that cling to water lilies. Only by education can children be prevented from bathing in any of Africa's quiet, beautiful, yet dangerous pools. If given a chance, the parasites become attached to a human, penetrating the skin and lodging in the liver. Being a bilharzia victim is not fatal, but having the complaint makes a person chronically tired. Field teams cut away the foliage that grows in pools, and spray the water with a copper sulphate solution. This treatment has only a slight effect on the parasite, for bilharzia is a tough disease to combat.

The third important category in the plan is special care for children and advice to their mothers. By 1974, it is expected that 275 Rural Health Clinics will be in operation, each to cater to fifty thousand people. These centers will prescribe certain diets for children and special care for infant complaints. The attendants encourage women to come regularly for prenatal checkups and to attend planned parenthood discussion groups. One voluntary organization helps families in spacing their children. The Family Planning Association of Tanzania was formed in 1959

and became affiliated with International Planned Parenthood in
1965. Mrs. Christins Nsekela, the executive secretary of the association, explains that the need is to curb the mortality of infants
and young children and to protect the health of mothers by having them space their babies. Membership in the association increases rapidly, as much as three times in a year, as Tanzania's
motto becomes more widely used—"Fewer but healthier babies."

Both the British Medical Research Council and the World
Health Organization give practical support to Tanzania's Ministry of Health's plan to gain control of communicable diseases
through research and a program of regular vaccinations.

Every town in Tanzania has a modern hospital for easing the
suffering of the afflicted. In Dar es Salaam one large five-hun-
dred-bed hospital has in addition dental and outpatients' clinics.
And new hospitals are in the process of being built in Dodoma,
Moshi, and Mwanza. But as it is with the dispensaries and rural
health centers, the personnel of every hospital faces the challeng-
ing task of handling more patients than a hospital can accommodate.

When the preventive sickness battle is won, then the strain on
Tanzania's hospitals will be eased. And with good health come
happiness and strengthened ability for the task of building a nation.

10

Transportation

Mwalimu Nyerere, acutely aware of his people's nutritional lack, once said, "If we produce more meat people can have a better diet. To catch more fish will improve their health."

Improved foods were being produced more plentifully. Meats were of a higher quality in areas of the country where cattle thrived. All sorts of edible fish, large and small, abounded in Lakes Tanganyika and Victoria. But what advantage was there in having a farmer improve his crops, a cattleman his herds, and for a fisherman to use larger and stronger nets to catch more fish? Without a means of conveying the good merchandise to markets it often became a total loss, and subsequently the producers were plagued with a sense of failure. Tanzania's few roads were in a deplorable condition, and the railroads the Germans had built sixty years previously had deteriorated over the years.

An important project in Tanzania's second Five-Year-Plan, started in 1969, was to construct new arteries and to rebuild already existing roads, poor though they were. The plan was allocated about one-third of Tanzania's total financial resources. Priority was given to work on the trunk roads. Three main north-south roads and four running east-west were designed to connect all parts of the country, including the nine newly developed townships.

Another ambitious plan, undertaken jointly by Tanzania and Zambia, Tanzania's neighbor to the west, was to build a road connecting Dar es Salaam with Lusaka, Zambia's capital. Loans were secured from Sweden and the United States who saw that

The Tanzania Zambia Railway as it surges ahead from Dar es Salaam to Kapiri Mposhi.

the building of the road was an emergency for Zambia, a land-locked country in dire need of an access to the sea through a friendly country. Zambia borders Rhodesia, the white-controlled land to her south, and Angola, the Portuguese province to her west. For Tanzania, the link by road with Zambia held promising trade potentials.

Tanzam, as the road is called, will measure 1,256 miles long, 622 miles of which will cross Tanzanian territory. Part of the construction goes through terrain never before surveyed. Starting in Dar es Salaam the tarmac-surfaced road will cut between a housing development on the city's western limits, then proceed to Morogoro and to Mikumi in hilly country where to make passage possible a way is being hewn through living rock.

At Iringa the road connects with the old Great North Road which in recent years earned the name of Hell Run. Few cars succeeded in getting through without being repeatedly mired axle-deep in mud. Abandoned cars were landmarks on the gruesome stretch between Iringa, Mbeya, and Tunduma, a town on the Zambian border. In the rainy season the old 633-mile-long road from Tunduma to Lusaka was, if possible, even muddier than the stretch on the Tanzanian side. On the whole it was a lonely road through wild but beautiful Zambian country.

Rains have delayed the scheduled completion of Tanzam. When finished, however, the road will be more than an exit route for Zambia. It will be a two-way international trade route.

Work on the local roads proceeds as scheduled though one necessary connection between Dar es Salaam and the cashew nut center, Mtwara, which was intended to follow the coast southward, has been postponed. The expense of building a road across the Rufiji Delta runs so high that the project is not feasible. In-

Instead of running up and down steep slopes, the railroad track will cross the valley on a bridge. The pillars that will support the bridge are shown in preparation.

stead a new coastal shipping line operates between Dar es Salaam, Mtwara, and several offshore islands. The Norwegian government provided shipping experts and manned one ship for the line which is a subsidiary of Tanzania's National Transport Corporation.

Dar es Salaam's harbor facilities are being expanded. When the work is completed on seven new deep water berths by the mid-1970's, Dar es Salaam will have ten deep water berths and, outside the harbor, a new mooring device for tankers.

In 1968, two years after Rhodesia's Unilateral Declaration of Independence and Zambia's isolation from independent countries, a temporary airlift operation began for flying oil to Zambia's copper mines. The same year the Italian government aided the building of an oil pipeline between Dar es Salaam and Ndola, a town in the heart of Zambia's Copperbelt. An average of three hundred thousand tons of refined oil has since been pumped through annually.

The pipeline and the Tanzam road are two links Tanzania has with Zambia. The third link, a colossal undertaking, is scheduled for completion in 1975. It is *Tanzara*, the Tanzania-Zambia railroad. The railroad will give Zambia access to seaports rather than have her annual export of nearly eight hundred thousand tons of copper carried through Rhodesia and Mozambique to Beira on the east coast.

The idea of linking Tanzania and Zambia by railroad materialized some years ago. The United States was approached for financial aid but said the project would be too costly. The World Bank rejected the suggestion, stating that even if the train carried all the copper traffic outward, it would have little to bring back. A United Nations report described the project as speculative.

It was a surprise, then, when the People's Republic of China came forward with a generous proposal. They would not only finance a railroad, but would build it. In September, 1967, a tripartite agreement was signed in Peking. In 1968 the Chinese started a two-year survey of the railbed, and in 1970 the three parties concerned, Tanzania, Zambia, and the Chinese Republic, reached an agreement. China would advance a loan, interest-free, amounting to $401.2 million. Repayments of the loan would commence in 1983 and extend over thirty years.

Work on the railroad had already started by October, 1970, when President Kenneth Kaunda of Zambia laid a foundation stone at the commencement of the 1,166-mile-long tracks. Present at the ceremony in Dar es Salaam were President Nyerere and Mr. Fang-Yi, the Chinese minister for the Commission of Economic Affairs with Foreign Countries.

About thirteen thousand Chinese workers, including forty-seven hundred technicians and engineers, were put to work on the construction of workshops, bridges, tunnels, and embankments. The first completed projects were the Chinese personnel reception center at Kurasini near Dar es Salaam and, adjacent to it, a fully equipped medical center staffed by Chinese. Rolling stock repair shops, a stores depot, and major base camps were set up at strategic places along the route. A sawmill yard was built at one base and logs were brought from a nearby forest and sawn into timber for making the ties.

Another base included the mixing of cement for four large and nineteen small bridges, and countless culverts. Bulldozers, excavators, and dredges leveled or removed hills. Farther along the line a second hospital, served by a medical staff of twenty-two Chinese doctors and nurses, is equipped with an X-ray unit, operating theater, laboratory, pharmacy, dental and eye units. The total labor force numbers about fifty thousand.

The builders of Tanzara face a tremendous challenge, for they have to combat a difficult terrain and sometimes unexpected weather problems. In the beginning, in low-lying areas subject to heavy rains, work had to be performed in shifts on embankments, culverts, and bridges.

A train starts in Dar es Salaam and has an even run along the coastal plains until it meets the escarpment leading up to the highlands. Climbing this treacherous stretch means twisting and turning around precipitous curves. The train then winds its way through and around the Southern Highlands in comparative ease until it comes to the Zambian plain which in some places is

A passenger car is parked at the side of Kisawasawa (Mang'ula) Station as a cargo train passes along with a cargo of construction timber.

several hundred feet high and in others only a few feet above sea level. Numerous big and small rivers and swamps are crossed before the train reaches its destination in Kapiri Mposhi, Zambia.

For Tanzania, Tanzara offers limitless advantages. It will justify its existence by solving Zambia's transportation problems, but it will also open Tanzania's Southern Highlands regions which are potentially rich but out of the mainstream of communications—a prime factor in development.

Southern Tanzania was rumored as being rich in iron and coal, a rumor that was recently verified by Chinese surveyors. The railroad will no doubt be instrumental in opening Tanzania's steel and coal industries.

But the farmers will benefit the most, for the train will pass through tobacco and coffee country and across the wide Rufiji valley and its rice fields. Already farmers are enriched by trade with Chinese workers along the line. Never before have they sold in such volume and so consistently.

Building the railroad has provided employment for seven thousand young Tanzanians. They have practical experience in the work camps and when they have mastered the operating of machines Chinese instructors give them theoretical training. This industrial training prepares young men for future responsibilities. No doubt that from their numbers there will emerge leaders to guide an industrialized Tanzania into prosperity.

Tanzania's people have reasons for rejoicing. They can already see that improved transportation means a livelier trade which is bringing them the material benefits for which they yearn.

11

Industry

Tanzania is quickly becoming an industrialized nation, but foreign currency is a vital need if TANU's ambitious plan is to succeed. More commodities have to be sold overseas in order to finance the importation of equipment such as machinery and certain raw materials for Tanzania's new industries which are expected to expand along with the country's growth.

Under the direction of the National Development Corporation, 350 industrial projects are in process of development which will raise the contribution to Tanzania's economy from 8 percent in 1969 to an expected sevenfold increase by 1985. Turning to industry is a part of nation-building. For Tanzania it is becoming a necessity as overseas demands lessen for some of her agricultural products.

Tanzania's main exports are coffee, cotton, sisal, and diamonds. Ujamaa villagers heeded Mwalimu Nyerere's advice to "produce more sisal, cotton, and coffee to sell overseas to buy things we want," and the production of these commodities increased. But even to Nyerere it was unforeseen that the price of coffee would decline on the world market. Coffee is the main cash crop for many thousands of farmers. In the Kilimanjaro district alone 105,420 farmers cultivating 65,320 acres produced 17,022 tons of coffee in one year. Their situation could become a predicament if competition from other developing countries continues to influence the drop in coffee prices. Tanzania, not being a major producer of coffee, has little control over the fluctuation in price. But a suggested solution to the problem is to gradually reduce coffee growing and convert to more remunerative products such as tea and dairy products.

NDC is supervising the improvement in Tanzania's tea with the intention of increasing overseas sales. Already more than half of the tea exported is shipped to North America and western Europe, and as the quality is sampled and proved satisfactory, no doubt the export of this commodity will increase.

Milk, butter, and cheese have until now been bought from Kenya. By installing modern equipment, Tanzania will be able to satisfy the entire nation's dairy products needs.

Sisal growers face the same problem as do coffee growers. Other developing countries are selling sisal on the world market where there is less demand than formerly. To meet the deficit, Tanzania has turned to manufacturing its own transporting bales and twines from sisal.

By contrast, Tanzania's cotton is a burgeoning market that is expected to expand, and three large textile mills manufacture all of the country's textile needs. Because Tanzanian cotton is of a superior grade, it is exported to all parts of the world including the Far East. For every 100 bales produced in 1969, it is estimated that 152 bales of raw cotton will be produced in 1974.

NDC and Nyanza Cooperative Union each hold 40 percent of the shares in one new mill situated in Mwanza. Amenital, a

Processed fibers of sisal, country's leading crop, being laid out to dry.
Uluguru Mountains are in background.

French company representing the technical consultants, holds
the remaining 20 percent. At the Mwanza Textile Company, as
it is called, twelve hundred employees work full time and produce 24 million yards of cotton yard goods annually.

Another enterprise with a promising future is cigarettes. Although only one million of Tanzania's 7 million adults are smok-
ers, one new factory in Dar es Salaam could not keep pace with
the demand for their certain brand. After one month in operation the company was compelled to order larger machinery. Tobacco growers along Lake Victoria's western shore produce the

Cotton, Tanzania's second most important crop, is picked (*above*) and carried to buying post (*below*) on Ukerewe Island.

most popular type of tobacco for cigarettes that are exported in quantity. Locally, they are distributed through ujamaa shops.

There is a food that is full of nutrition and good to chew. Everyone eats it but few people know the long process it goes through before being ready to serve on ice cream or in cakes, or just to be eaten by itself. This is the cashew nut. It is a huge foreign currency earner, for Tanzania exports over one hundred thousand tons of raw nuts every year. The cashew industry is a big business that will grow even bigger.

At present about 20 percent of the nuts are processed in Tanzania—at Dar es Salaam and at Mtwara the nut-growing center. But as more companies set up the machinery, the more the finished product will be completed in Tanzania.

In former years all the nuts were sent to India where through practice the women are quick and skillful at shelling, peeling, and sorting them by hand. This is the first stage in preparation.

Inventors have tried by mechanical means to duplicate the level of perfection attained by the experts. One Italian method is to roast the nuts in a hot oil bath—of course after they have been cleaned, graded, and had all foreign matter removed. The Japanese developed another mechanical method called the cold process whereby the nuts are steamed to make their shells brittle and easy to remove.

Both Italian and Japanese companies have built plants in Tanzania in partnership with NDC. The combined production of "hot" and "cold" methods will eventually yield some fifty thousand tons of processed cashews a year, giving employment to thousands of people. And as an aid to out of the way ujamaa villages, a few processing units are operated jointly by NDC and the villagers.

As a sort of bonus, one by-product of cashews that is gaining popularity on world markets is the nutshell liquid which is used in paints, automobile brake linings, and in resins. Such good business brings happiness to the people of Mtwara, an area of the country that is far removed from the mainstream of activity.

To the west of Mtwara is Mbeya, a town conveniently located beside the Tanzara railroad for one new enterprise. Employees of the Mbeya abattoirs turn cattle into beef, prepare it for the markets, and ship the frozen meat over the Tanzam road to all sections of Tanzania.

The hides are tanned for making bags and belts and footwear. After enlarging its premises and installing new machinery, one NDC company increased the production of leather shoes from 2 million to 3 million, which was sufficient to meet half of Tanzania's footwear requirements.

For some years the Tanganyika Packers Company has exported canned foods. Canned corn, grapefruit and grapefruit juice, tomatoes and baked beans, have been found on many foreign dinner tables. Luscious mangoes, picked when ripe, then canned, are a popular export delicacy. Now, the government assists in marketing the products of small-scale factories which have been set up in a number of ujamaa villages for canning fruits, vegetables, and jams to augment the village income.

Tanzania's government also makes sure that cottage industries are encouraged in ujamaa villages. It provides the training for artisans in occupations such as metalwork and woodwork, pottery and household utensils. One popular outlet for the beautiful articles villagers make is the National Small Industries Corporation in Dar es Salaam. The NSIC is a busy center. In addition to handling the contributions from rural workers, the shop maintains 140 units with four hundred artisans who include furniture and dyed cloth among a variety of unique creations.

It is no surprise that with the big spurt in industry Tanzania should experience a building boom. For a while the supply of building materials could not keep pace with demand. The deficiency was particularly noticeable in the production of cement. Tanzania's one company, the Tanzania Portland Cement Company, produced 169,637 tons of cement in 1969 but it was not enough for Tanzania's growing needs. So the company built new factories and by the end of 1971 was producing 400,000 tons of cement. A study is now being carried out by NDC for a new cement plant in the vicinity of Tanga where limestone is plentiful.

Steel that is required in building was scarce until a new steel-rolling mill at Tanga started to operate. Its capacity is thirty thousand tons of rolled products annually, which supply window frames, iron bars, flats and angles for Tanzania's new constructions.

Less conspicuous but equally as important is the manufacture of farm implements. Formerly, farmers' tools were imported, but through the efforts of Mr. Kawawa, the Ubungo Farm Implement Manufacturing Company was set up with the aid of technical experts from the People's Republic of China. The jembe— meaning "hoe"—that is the symbol of Tanzanian self-reliance is now made to the number of three hundred thousand each year. And plows designed to be drawn by oxen are made in lots of three thousand. With such simple yet vital tools, the peasant farmer can vastly improve the quality and quantity of his crops.

Dense green forests cover the Usambara Highlands in northern Tanzania. They are the source for sawn timber, chipboard, and sawmill factories a mile down the mountainside. And a hardwood mill, started near Tabora, makes railroad ties for reconstructing old East African railroads. Research is in progress as to the possibility of using Tanzanian wood for making paper, and if this proves successful one essential import will be eliminated.

But there is an awareness of the necessity for conservation in a land with a rising population whose resources must be cherished. The development program includes the planting of new forests. And forestry and agricultural experts advise the people in villages and schools on the need to plan ahead. They assist them in starting plantations of their own for future use.

Tanzanians have the visible proof that the energy they apply to developing industry is valuable. Where there were forty thousand industrial workers in 1969, the figure is expected to increase to sixty thousand by 1974. Workers are imbued with *Jenga*, which is the Swahili word meaning "to build." The word is being put to its full use in a country of people dedicated to reaching the goal of complete independence.

12

Natural Resources

An industry that could be Tanzania's biggest project is being investigated now, but even if the reports are optimistic several years will pass before the project is built and reaches a workable condition. If the estimated thousands of tons of iron ore and coal deposits made by Chinese engineers while in southern Tanzania are close to reality, total industrialization would follow almost immediately with the assembling of equipment and opening of the mines. The project involves the mining of iron and coal for manufacturing steel—at present an expensive import item.

All sorts of metallurgical analyses are being made on the iron ore in a search for other possible mineral contents, and a fuel research unit at the University of Dar es Salaam is examining coal samples to determine, among other experiments, if they are of a quality for making coke.

Should the project materialize, a town to accommodate thirty thousand people will be built; four thousand people will be employed to construct a steel mill, and two thousand to run it.

The mill will operate in conjunction with Tanzara, the new

railroad, loading the train with freight not only for new constructions in Tanzania, but for Zambia as well.

Most mining in Tanzania is on a small scale. Gold is practically worked out, but some silver, tin, tungsten, gypsum, mica, and magnesite are still mined on a small scale. Of limestone there is plenty, recently uncovered deposits being found near the iron ore site. Salt production has risen since the solar evaporation process was introduced. Evaporation in tanks as large as lakes takes about four months, but enough salt is gleaned to fill Tanzania's needs for this indispensable commodity and to supply neighboring countries.

Tanzania's fourth main foreign currency earner, diamonds, is still the leading nonagricultural profit maker in the NDC group of companies. The average size of individual mined diamonds had decreased in 1969, but Williamson Company Limited reported that the company made a profit because of a market price increase. Close to $3\frac{1}{2}$ million tons of ore were mined and 731,294 carats extracted, a big increase in volume over the preceding year.

NDC holds 75 percent of the shares of the company which has three subsidiaries and together with free-lance prospectors employs 2,109 persons. The diamonds are sent to London in lots where they are sorted by the Tanzania Diamond Sorting Organization. Some diamonds are returned to Tanzania for cutting and polishing by the Tanzania Diamond Cutting Company.

The discovery of diamonds near Mwadui in the Shinyanga region makes an exciting story. The discoverer was Dr. John T. Williamson who was born in Quebec, Canada, in 1907. But after winning his diploma as a mining engineer from McGill University, Williamson sailed off to South Africa.

John Williamson followed a strong hunch that diamonds were buried somewhere in East Africa, but other mining engineers scoffed at the suggestion. So Williamson set off to prospect alone, first in Zambia, then in Tanzania. He looked for the blue clay, the end product of volcanic stone that has crumbled away, where diamonds are found. Every day for many months Williamson searched by digging and sieving the earth. He was sick and hungry most of the time but tenaciously kept on digging. Africans who watched as he worked named him "The White Man Without Luck."

It was on a rainy day in 1940 that Williamson found diamonds. His old car had sunk to the axles in the muddy bed of a stream, and when he tried to free the vehicle with his hands, groping in the mud around the wheels, Williamson saw that they were covered with blue clay. He searched frantically in the bed of the stream and at last felt what he was looking for—diamonds. Filling a small bag with a few samples, Williamson begged a lift from a passing hunter. The man obligingly drove Williamson to the District Officer in Tabora to register his claim.

Williamson built a model town far out in the country beside his diamond mine. In time he became one of the richest men in the world and when asked how he intended spending his fortune answered, "A fortune is only what one does with it." He continued providing comfort for his workers until his death in 1958 at the age of fifty. Mourned by his thousands of workers, Williamson remained to them "The White Man Without Luck."

During the thirty years since Williamson's discovery, a total of 10.8 million carats (2.4 tons) of diamonds have been extracted from 40 million tons of gravel. The world's largest pink diamond accounted for $54\frac{1}{2}$ carats of the total. After the two years necessary to cut the stone to its present exquisite form it weighed 24 carats. Williamson had the gem set, then he gave it as a wedding present to Britain's Princess Elizabeth, now the Queen.

Diamond mining is declining in Tanzania, but semiprecious stones are on the uprise in popularity and contribute enormous wealth to the economy. Most of the world's gems are found in Tanzania, but a newly discovered stone, fitly known as *Tanzanite*, is entirely Tanzanian. The beautiful blue zoisite stone was first discovered in 1967 near Arusha. Though they are still mined rather primitively, by 1970 tanzanites accounted for more than half the value of all gemstone exports.

When NDC's plan to find a working partner materializes and production is more rapid, the stone, compounded of calcium and aluminum, will be a major export.

Just as the people are important in furthering development, so is utilizing natural resources part of Tanzania's overall nation-building plan.

13

Artists and Their Works

President Nyerere listened with deep concern to young people playing pianos when they should have been learning the marvelous rhythms of drumbeats. He shuddered as he watched dancers perform imported "twists" and "rock 'n' roll" while dressed in eccentric Western clothing. A borrowed culture seemed to be taking hold and Tanzania's unique art heritage was sinking into oblivion under the impact and influence of a Western culture.

Mwalimu Nyerere decided to include a Ministry of National Culture in his first cabinet, formed soon after independence. And he spoke strongly against the effect of this intrusion on his country's youth in one address he gave, saying, "A country which lacks its own culture is no more than a collection of people without the spirit which makes them a nation." So he and the government set about making vigorous efforts to preserve and to promote Tanzania's rare and inspiring arts.

Students who possess talents in any branch of the arts are encouraged to enroll for training with the University of Dar es Salaam which maintains departments in the performing, fine, and graphic arts, sculpture, music, and literature.

One dance group, trained in the Department of Theater Arts at the university, performs both traditional and modern African dances—which are modern only in a sense that an arranger had adapted ancient dances to conform to contemporary preferences. Performing with the dancers are master drummers who use either the tall drums with one end covered with parchment, or massive hollowed logs. The former type they pound with their

Members of UWT, the national women's organization, perform a traditional dance at National Stadium to mark Tanzania Union Day.

hands, the latter with heavy sticks. Both types of drums resonate with great vibrating rhythms. Dancers respond to the compelling staccato rhythm of the drums with wild leaps and turns, or with gentle gyrations. They will flutter their hands high above their heads, then suddenly bend and touch them to the ground. Musicians using other indigenous instruments also accompany the dancers, or a singer may accompany herself on a zeze, a traditional stringed instrument that resembles a banjo. The marimba, which is like a small xylophone but with metal rather than wooden bars, is one East African instrument that has found popularity in countries beyond Africa.

The same university dance group traveled with members of the Tanzania Dance Company—TDC—to Japan's Expo '70 as a special delegation led by Mr. Rashidi Kawawa. When the dancers performed seemingly impossible feats of tumbling and somersaulting the audience stood to applaud them.

Some of Tanzania's most talented musicians and dancers are with the TDC. One blind entertainer, Morris Nyunyusa, plays on ten drums at once with only slight assistance from his wife and young son. His performance was chosen to be recorded, and the tape is played as an identifying feature between Radio Tanzania programs.

Snake dancing was a dying art until it was revived by the TDC. The poisonous snakes that the dancers twine around their heads and bodies are frightening to behold until audiences are assured that the snakes have been doped with certain powerful drugs. It is a dancer's exclusive duty to care for his particular reptile—collecting the herbs himself, preparing the medicine, and administering it.

Stilt dancing is a second unique performance that has been

saved from extinction by national efforts. No more than six eld-
erly men remained who could perform this intricate balancing
act with their legs tightly bound to ten-foot-tall stilts. The dance
appeared only on ceremonial occasions in traditional rituals.
These Makonde tribesmen presented an awesome spectacle as
they strode around the arena with their bodies painted white,
and with black plumes swaying from their hair. Today, younger
Makonde men recognize the value of stilt dancing as a rich Tanzanian heritage and accept instruction from their elders.

The Makonde are an inventive group of Bantu who inhabit
the coastal areas of southern Tanzania. Tribal groups throughout the country practice the art of wood carving, making bowls
and spoons and other utilitarian articles, but the Makonde are
the only people in Tanzania who utilize the human form in their
designs. The more talented carvers create groupings of several
figures in involved attitudes and intertwinings. The results are
magnificent examples of fine ebony wood carving.

In 1970 the National Arts of Tanzania became incorporated
with the National Development Corporation. The company acts
as the artists' agent, arranging exhibits for selling their works and
ensuring them a generous share of the sales. Makonde carvings
are in demand, and many pieces are sold for export through the
National Arts of Tanzania Corporation. One foremost Makonde
carver, Pajume Alale, is satisfied with the financial arrangement.
Not having to sell his own creations leaves him more time for his
work, he says, and time to contribute to the life of his village.
Though famous as a creative carver, Pajume Alale does his share
of tilling the soil and sowing the seed.

Artists who graduate from schools of fine arts have their
paintings displayed as murals in many of Tanzania's new build-

ings, and as pictures on the walls of offices and homes. There are pictures that are abstract in design, and others that are representational. All are original in conception, and are portrayed with strong contrasting colors that show a Tanzanian's appreciation for and knowledge of the use of color.

The same bold treatment with color is evident in Tanzania's textile designing, a comparatively new art form. In two textile mills that NDC partly owns, the management employs artists who adapt traditional symbols to their designs. The designers visit museums to study specimens of ancient arts that are preserved in all sorts of articles their ancestors used or wore. Old paintings on bark, ear plugs, and early examples of Makonde carvings, for instance, are the inspirations for stars, scrolls, stripes, and spirals that later appear on cotton materials. The artists favor vivid gold, greens, and blacks, which are the colors used in Tanzania's national flag.

The beauty of printed fabrics from Tanzania's textile mills enhances dance performances, for the dancers wear in their costumes only the materials that are created by their own country's artists and designers.

There are media through which Tanzania's dancing and visual arts are promoted. Several papers and magazines in the Swahili language, and two English-language daily newspapers, *The Standard* and *The Nationalist*, report news pertaining to the arts. The written word attracts attention when journalists write unbiased, truthful criticisms of current art shows and dance performances. People who are learning to understand that Tanzanian culture can enrich their lives read the reports, then flock to share the beauty of inanimate objects on display, whether they are sculptures or one of the month-long exhibits that NDC arranges on the first floor of its main office in Dar es Salaam.

The NDC exhibitions provide an opportunity to display in separate booths, the merchandise from NDC's various associate companies. It is not unusual for a plastics merchant to have his stand next to, say, that of the Tanzanian Publishing House, Limited.

This publishing company is bringing pressure on increasing the use of the Swahili language. Though its editors publish a few books in English, they are turning more to Swahili manuscripts, encouraging writers to use the language that is recognized as being national, therefore part of Tanzania's culture. The Tanzanian Publishing House publishes the Swahili textbooks used in elementary schools. They will also publish the textbooks for high schools as the language is more widely adopted. Included in the company's list are English books translated into Swahili. The works of William Shakespeare are among them, an innovation that is readily endorsed by Mwalimu Nyerere who uses his spare time in also translating Shakespeare's plays into Swahili.

The Tanzanian Publishing House extended its publications into the field of general interest when it produced *Private Enterprise and the East African Company*, a book in English that has worldwide value to everyone who follows Tanzania's remarkable progress in nation-building.

A second publishing house, the East African, chooses authors who handle the pains and problems of transition. Two books by Okot p'Bitek are controversial. The first of his books, *Song of Lawino*, pleads for the traditional life, whereas his second book, *Song of Ocol*, presents arguments that support modern living. As one book is a sequel of the other, the publisher recommends that both books be read together to fully appreciate the pros and cons of a situation that many Tanzanians find puzzling.

Talented poets and short-story writers usually prefer Swahili as their medium of expression. Mathias Mnyampala was one gifted poet who adapted an ancient traditional form of poetry to modern needs. It was a great loss to the country when he died in 1969. But a new troupe of graduate writers from the Institute of Education at the University of Dar es Salaam are producing short stories and plays which the National Service of Radio Tanzania broadcasts regularly.

Great strides have been achieved in making the people "culture-conscious" since independence, but Mwalimu Nyerere was not satisfied. Under the direction of his brother, Joseph Nyerere, secretary-general of the Youth League, a campaign got under way in 1969 to rid the country of "imported corruptions."

"Tanzanian youths must do away with these obscene foreign influences," said Joseph Nyerere as he organized Operation Vijana (*Vijana* meaning youths) into parties of patrols. With the aid of posters, the Vijana set out to eliminate miniskirts, skin bleaches, wigs, and hair straighteners. They ordered boys to discard their too tight or bell-bottomed pants, too wide belts, flamboyant ties, and ten-gallon hats. The Vijana made some impression and a report came from Tanga that girls had publicly burned their miniskirts.

In Dar es Salaam, Coast Regional Commissioner Songambele placed a ban on "soul" music in Tanzania's capital. *The Standard* printed an editorial that "Soul music . . . was an invitation to decadence and the worst type of Afro-American importation, owing nothing to the spiritualist origins of the Deep South plantation music . . ." *The Nationalist* daily newspaper wrote that "Soul digging is the worst kind of deception, dupery, stultification, and corruption of the youth. It must go."

The "West" has always had a great influence throughout East

Africa. This is particularly noticeable in the manner of dress, and in education. But TANU officials observe a strict, almost puritanical, attitude toward personal behavior. It was partly the introduction of modern Western trends, the Tanzanian resolve to work out its own destiny, and a reduced demand for teachers that brought about the expulsion of Peace Corps workers in December of 1967.

Perhaps, given the time, Tanzania's people will return to wearing their graceful kanzu entirely, made of fine cotton and patterned with striking nationalist designs.

But there will always be some foreign influence to combat as more and more visitors come to view what beautiful Tanzania has to show them. And no doubt the tourists will be wearing the latest-style Western fashions.

14

Beyond the Cities

Each year increasing numbers of visitors flock to share the diversity of pleasures that Tanzania offers. Whereas in 1966 an estimated 45,280 outsiders toured Tanzania, by 1974 their numbers are expected to have increased to a yearly total of 100,000. The National Development Corporation knows that visitors bring revenue to the country, so tourism is a major part of the nation's building program.

Visitors to Tanzania for the first time are surprised when they see the bustle and excitement of the cities, the commodious hotels to welcome them, and the evidence of activity in the industrial areas that skirt them. They are delighted with the exhibits of paintings, weaving, pottery, and Makonde carvings displayed for their choice as lasting mementos of an unforgettable holiday.

Though visits to ujamaa villages are banned to tourists for security reasons, other unique activities are waiting beyond the cities. Some visitors seek the serenity of wooded hillsides overlooking wide undulating plains while others accept the challenges offered by mountain climbing and deep-sea fishing. But everyone shares the excitement of viewing Tanzania's wildlife, more closely concentrated than anywhere else on earth.

At the time of independence Tanzania had one wild-game reserve, Serengeti, whose 5,700 square miles extend from the eastern shore of Lake Victoria to the Ngorongoro Crater and Masailand, the home of Masai warriors. Today there are seven national parks, each containing its characteristic flora and fauna.

Serengeti is probably the most spectacular of the parks with at least thirty-five different kinds of wild animals and ten times as many birds. Handsome black-maned lions stroll in prides across the plains, or doze in the shadows cast by acacia trees. Sometimes a pride of lions will climb the trees to avoid pesky flies, and sprawl along the branches while taking their siestas. Herds of striped zebra move within sight, indifferent to the lions' presence when they sense the beasts have eaten. Browsing giraffes pluck leaves from the treetops, and from the rim of forests the king of land mammals, the elephant, snaps off trees with sounds as sharp as gunshots. An elephant can easily uproot a tree by pushing at it with his forehead and huge forelegs. With the tree flat on its side, the herd gathers to feast off the tender topmost leaves.

Warthogs keep themselves aloof from other animals, but they are a common sight, trotting Indian-style across the plains with the mother warthog leading the way. Her four to six young ones follow with their bristly little tails carried straight up like antennae. A warthog is far from handsome, having beady eyes and ugly warts all over a head that seems too big for a tubby body. Businesslike tusks turn upward from a wide mouth. When sounds of snuffling and scuffling come from the underbrush it means that the warthog is rooting up some succulent morsel for her family's dinner.

Giraffe and rhinoceroses make a rare group in Momella National Park near Arusha.

Warthogs are as common as sparrows in a park, but one rare species, the Giant Forest Hog, was recently seen for the first time in Serengeti, and for the second time in all of Tanzania.

Tanzania is rich in the variety and number of its antelope. They frequent the parks in thousands, from the giant eland to small antelope no bigger than rabbits. The most graceful of the antelope are the impala who travel in herds and spring through the air, up and down, like horses on a carousel.

The lakes in park reserves buzz with animal and bird life. Hippopotomuses blow bubbles, snort, and frolic in the shallow water. Crocodiles lie as motionless as logs, their little eyes seemingly closed but really alert for some unsuspecting prey to venture near their snapping jaws. Immense ungainly rhinoceroses forage in the underbrush. Foraging is a rhino's constant occupation for his

Wildebeest in Serengeti National Park inside vast Ngorongoro Crater.

daily consumption of fodder adds up to some five hundred pounds.

Leopards use high branches as storage places for their kill. They will drag a fair-sized carcass to a spot sometimes thirty feet above the reach of scavenging animals such as hyenas, jackals, and wild dogs. The leopard is only one of several spotted cats in East Africa, but he is easily the most cunning as he slinks through the grasses in his sleek yellow coat patterned in brown circular spots. Leopards are legally protected against capture, one of the reasons being that they are ruthlessly hunted for their handsome coats and like many other African species, are threatened with

Cheetah.

extinction. A second reason for protecting leopards is their success in keeping the baboon population in check. Baboons are regarded as being man's public enemy number one. They are destructive to crops, and overnight will strip a cornfield bare, plucking the cobs and scattering them, and tearing apart the cornstalks.

Big brown baboons swagger around a picnic site and unless sharply discouraged, will snatch a sandwich from a picnicker's hand before he can take a bite. Whereas vervet monkeys wearing soft gray and white fur, merely chatter as a harmless warning to intruders.

Chimpanzees make their homes in the Tarangire Park near Arusha. They are under the constant observation of scientists who study their habits to help determine what exactly is the level of intelligence of these close-to-human primates.

Over one thousand different species of birds, most of them migratory, add their songs to the barks and snarls and roars of animals. And like the animals, they descend on water holes and the banks of streams in the early evening. Tens of thousands of pink flamingos stand wing to wing in the shallows of lakes that are alkaline. Lake Manyara is noted for the density of its flamingos. If they are suddenly startled the birds take flight and their pink turns to the color of strawberry jam, for underneath a flamingo's wings the color deepens.

The world's biggest bird, the ostrich, stalks majestically across the plains in a search for new grasses or tiny buds. An ostrich is a vegetarian though he gulps down pebbles on occasion as an aid to his digestion.

An ostrich cannot fly, but a secretary bird can, though awkwardly. He is as dignified as an ostrich when strutting in search

Hippos with the young one ready for a dip in Momella National Park.

of food, but he is no vegetarian. A secretary bird relishes snakes and lizards, slimy grubs, and snails. He considers a small turtle a special delicacy. A secretary bird looks like an old-time secretary, and that is how he got his name. Long black quills jut backward from just above his ears. The secretary bird belongs to the eagle family with a wingspread of seven feet. He roosts at night on a large platform on the top of a tree. The nest needs to be broad for the young birds dare not leave the platform for fully six months, having spindly thin legs that are quite unsuited to face the hazards of a life on ground.

There is one East African bird that has a unique habit not practiced elsewhere. The honey guide, of the family Indicatoridae, likes beeswax in preference to honey. This little bird has developed a system over the centuries whereby he looks for the hives of wild bees, perhaps in a hollow log or hanging from a tree,

Chief Senge, the Regional Game Warden of Singida, feeds a young zebra which is to be sent to the new Saadani Game Park in Bagamoyo.

and having found one flies off in search of his partner—a honey badger, or ratel. The honey badger trots behind the bird until they come to the site of humming bees and dripping honey. He gets to work, and with long strong black claws, he tears at the hive, a thick skin and heavy fur being quite impervious to the attacks of angry bees. The honey guide waits at a safe distance and, only when the infuriated bees quiet down, joins the feast and gobbles up the wax while the ratel eats the honey.

This strange partnership has an additional feature. The honey guide uses the same tactics in seeking the help of humans, and African man aids this extraordinary bird also, following to wherever the bird may lead him.

But the bird's second mark of distinction is his ability to digest wax. Scientists study the phenomenon in efforts to identify some as yet unknown enzyme that makes the wax digestible, and if isolated will perhaps benefit mankind in combating the tuberculosis bacillus.

Being possessed of such extraordinary talents, one would expect the honey guide to be a bird of great beauty like many East African birds, but he is rather like an ordinary sparrow, though larger—just nondescript brownish-black with a yellow shoulder patch.

The Tanzania Tourist Board, a subsidiary of NDC, devises ingenious ways for making the viewing of wildlife easy. Good roads now link the seven reserves where comfortable hotels are established in each to cater to the wants of visitors. Some hotels have placed convenient platforms that overlook water holes where wildlife comes to drink at dusk. Park reserve officers leave molasses in troughs which act like magnets to all sorts of creatures, being so much tastier than old-fashioned salt-licks. Even lions

Elephants at Lake Manyara in the Northern Region. The hotel can be seen on top of the escarpment.

have been seen sampling the sticky sweetness of molasses.

NDC has established a new feature in wildlife conservation. It has built marine life reserves along sections edging the Indian Ocean where visitors may inspect the colorful coral reefs from specially designed boats.

Coral is a primitive marine animal which, when dead, is pushed upward as the new growth of live coral rises. At low tide only, the dead coral is visible. Sparkling with multicolored delicate tints, it is more beautiful dead than when it is alive.

There are numerous beaches washed by gentle waves that are good for wading in, or for swimming, or for goggling. Marine life reserves bring pleasure to visitors who enjoy the beauties of the seashore, but they have really been established to conserve Tan-

Mr. E. Kardelj, Yugoslav statesman on a visit, photographing buffaloes at the world-famous Lake Manyara National Park in the Northern Region of Tanzania.

zania's varieties of shells and water plants which are threatened with extinction because of indiscriminate collecting.

Some visitors look for activity more strenuous than swimming or examining the sea life. They hire boats for big game fishing. The Indian Ocean—the full length of Tanzania—teems with marlin, shark, tunny, and kingfish. Or a fisherman can cast his line from the shore or surf and haul in a fair-sized fish right there.

Tanzania's big lakes abound with perch and tiger fish, and the rivers that flow from Mount Kilimanjaro have trout.

Visitors looking for even hardier occupations turn to mountain climbing. Mount Kilimanjaro and its twin peak, Kibo, wait as perpetual challenges to intrepid climbers. There are several routes to follow. Some, tougher than others, require complete mountaineering gear for ascending sheer rock cliffs and for trudging through deep snowdrifts. A climber may chance to follow a course that takes him within sight of Tanzania's frozen leopard. At one time, no one knows when for sure, a leopard became wedged between rocks hundreds of feet above the timberline. He lies there still, encased in his frozen tomb.

The first ascent of Mount Kilimanjaro on record was made in 1889 by Professor Meyer, a German from Leipzig. Then in the early 1900's, Germans founded the Kilimanjaro Mountain Club. They built shelters, some of which still stand. Today, hotels at the foot of Mount Kilimanjaro organize five-day safaris up and down the mountain. And the Tanzania Tourist Board awards silver-plated plaques to those climbers who succeed in reaching Gillman's Point, 705 feet below the summit. But to climbers who reach the roof of Africa, Uhuru Point at 18,340 feet, the Tanzania Tourist Board awards gold-plated plaques. It was at Uhuru Point that the national flag was flown and bonfires lit on December 9, 1961, on the night of Independence Day. The generous recognition of achieving the heights is a strong inducement to potential climbers. Scores of people accept the challenge each year, though only a few take home a golden plaque.

Close attention is directed constantly toward making travel within Tanzania easier. Roads are better, railroads are extended and improved, planes from major European, Asian, and North

American airways fly to Dar es Salaam. Now, if they wish to, passengers can land in the vicinity of Mount Kilimanjaro. A lot of the credit for these advanced services goes to three East African countries, Tanzania, Uganda, and Kenya, whose leaders cooperate in the grand development plan called the East African Community.

15

The East African Community

No matter in which of the three countries a visitor's tour of East Africa starts, the three partner states in the East African Community—Tanzania, Uganda, and Kenya—combine their facilities in making travel comfortable and an exciting, memorable experience for strangers from overseas.

The East African Airways Corporation provides transportation for all of East Africa as well as operating domestic flights between the three countries. The East African Railways connects Tanzania, Uganda, and Kenya, and on stretches not covered by railroads, it runs bus services. The combined railroad also manages a luxury cruise that circles Lake Victoria. At 3,720 feet above sea level, visitors can relax for four days while they view the fishing and shoreline activities on and beside the lake. And there are trains waiting for disembarking passengers at Kisumu in Kenya, Mwanza in Tanzania, or Kampala in Uganda.

Catering to visitors is one facet of the many services rendered by the East African Committee of Planners which, by exchanging ideas and by experiment, makes maximum use of the three countries' most prominent points of interest.

One purpose of the East African Community, which was formed by the three Republics, is that the member states can sell freely to each other without the imposition of custom duties, and that as a community they can maintain a common external tariff.

In the years since the Treaty for East African Cooperation, which created the Community, was signed on June 6, 1967, at Kampala, and inaugurated at Arusha on December 1, 1967, the advantages of such a community are clearly evident. By strengthening and regulating their industrial, commercial, and other mutual interests such as tourism, the three countries are reaching a balanced development harmoniously.

The presidents of the three countries were the signatories to the Treaty—Mzee Kenyatta of Kenya, Mwalimu Nyerere of Tanzania, and Doctor Milton Obote of Uganda who is now in exile having been deposed, and replaced by General Idi Amin, in a military coup d'etat on January 25, 1971.

The three heads of state are known as the East African Authority which meets at least three times a year at the Central Secretariat in Arusha. Its duties are to guide and control the five executive functions of the Community, to settle problems unresolved in council meetings, and to approve certain appointments such as that of the secretary-general who is head of the Community's civil service and the Community's principal executive officer.

The five councils, each consisting of the three East African ministers and a varying number of national ministers from each of the partners, are classified as the Finance, Common Market, Economic Consultative and Planning, Communications, and Research and Social Councils.

The Community has four commercially run corporations for communications and harbor services. The corporations are the East African Airways and East African Railways with their head offices in Nairobi, the East African Harbors with its head office in Dar es Salaam, and the East African Telecommunications with its head office in Kampala. The last named not only links all parts of East Africa, but the rest of the world, by telephone, telegraph, cable, and postal services.

The Common Market Council handles matters pertaining to

Part of the Kilimanjaro International Airport building showing the control tower and an East African Airways plane.

industry and trade primarily. It also handles aviation and mete-orological services.

In the interests of industrial development, the Community established the East African Development Bank. Kenya, being the most advanced industrially, had an advantage until a readjustment allowed 38.75 percent of the bank's resources to be invested in both Uganda and Tanzania, and 22.5 percent in Kenya. Tanzania also reserved the exclusive right to supply the partner states with the assembling and manufacture of Land Rovers, one type of truck, tires, inner tubes, and radios. And to protect Tanzania's new factories, Uganda and Kenya agreed to increase their purchases of cement, knitwear, and tobacco from Tanzania, and to limit their exports to that country.

A transfer tax was established, also in the interest of maintaining a balanced industrial development, to be levied on manufactured goods leaving Kenya for either Uganda or Tanzania, or leaving Uganda for Tanzania. The tax system is reviewed from time to time, and is expected to be abolished by about 1980 when Tanzania has completed its industrialization.

The Customs and Excise Department assesses and collects the duty on all foreign merchandise entering the East African market, and collects excise on merchandise that is made locally for the three states. This department also levies a transfer tax on behalf of the government, and it enforces the laws pertaining to imported goods that are considered as being undesirable imports.

Only the partner states may refer their disputes to the Common Market Tribunal which was set up to ensure observances of the law and the terms of the treaty pertaining to the Common Market, though the Common Market Council has access to it on relevant matters. A Court of Appeals for East Africa with a president, vice-president, and justices of appeals, that is the highest appeals body in East Africa for criminal and civil cases, sits in Kampala, Nairobi, Mombasa, Zanzibar, and Dar es Salaam. An industrial court deals with all matters to do with salaries and working conditions of the Community and its four corporations.

An East African tax board advises the partner states on the correlation between taxes levied and managed by the Community and those levied directly and managed by the partner states. It keeps the administration of the Community customs and excise and income tax departments under review, including the allocation and distribution of revenues collected. The board must submit an annual report to the Finance Council.

The Community maintains twelve stations for research. Five stations are located in Kenya, three in Uganda, and four in Tanzania. To coordinate the two branches of research, medical and natural resources, there are two councils, each with a secretary and chairman. Industrial research is supervised by an industrial research board.

Impressive progress has been made in the field of medical research. Scientists working at the Institute of Medical Research in Mwanza are involved in efforts to eradicate bilharzia, the enervating disease that is carried by water snails. By isolating the snail vectors and improving insecticides to kill them, researchers are hopeful that this ancient disease, common to Africa, will be wiped out. The Tropical Pesticides Institute, in Arusha, is trying to improve insecticides which will eradicate pests that attack both humans and plants, including disease carriers like snails, tsetse flies, and mosquitoes. Near Tanga in Tanzania, the Institute of Malaria and Vector-Borne Diseases concentrates on controlling the spread of malaria.

In Nairobi, Kenya, the Tuberculosis Research Center has introduced a new treatment regime of unprecedented success even with advanced cases of the disease, and the Leprosy Research Center, also in Kenya, tests new drugs for use against the disease. The center maintains clinics where treatment is administered to sufferers.

The Trypanosomiasis Research Organization, in Uganda, is evolving methods to curb the development of sleeping sickness in humans and nagana in cattle which result from bites by tsetse flies. Tanzania has the biggest count of flies which have been found to breed in clumps of trees. Wild animals are immune to the fly's bite, otherwise the game reserves would not exist.

The Virus Research Institute, also in Uganda, wages a campaign against viruses, tiny infective agents that are responsible for spreading yellow fever, influenza, polio, smallpox, and chicken pox.

In the realm of natural resources, the Agriculture and Forestry Research Organization, Kenya, deals with improving East Africa's production of cash and food crops, both in their quality and quantity. In conjunction with National Agriculture and Forestry Ministries, the organization teaches how to grow healthier forests for timber.

In animal husbandry, the Veterinary Research Organization in Kenya concentrates on producing improved vaccines for use against various animal pestilences such as East Coast Fever and Rindepest, an infectious intestinal disease. The organization also experiments with the cross-breeding of local and imported animals.

A Marine Fisheries Research Organization in Zanzibar carries out research in all aspects of saltwater fishing off East Africa's coast. And the Freshwater Fisheries Research Organization keeps a check on the fish population and its abundance in all of East Africa's lakes as an aid to potential fish-canning industries in the partner states.

The good results of the East African Community's careful planning in each of its departments stand out as fine examples of cooperation between nations. Of course there have been instances when certain revisions and amendments were advisable, and these have been acted upon without friction.

The Community partly owes its success to the careful training of personnel in preparation for their different vocations. The East African Staff College gives last-stage training to officials for top management and administrative posts. The college aims its courses at the level of policy. Periodically, it brings together leading advisors from public and private sectors of the Community for continued discussion on possible policy changes they could apply in their daily work.

Four training schools operate within the General Fund Services of the Community. Secretarial colleges in Nairobi prepare personnel for specialized work, and the East African Statistical Training Center in Dar es Salaam supplies statistical information on a number of pertinent subjects. Trade, transport and communications, the whole range of banking and insurance, population, and employment, are among the subjects the training center teaches.

There is a school of aviation in Nairobi where young men train for air traffic control, radio maintenance, and telecommunication operations in preparation for posts in the various sections of the Directorate of Civil Aviation.

The Meteorological Training Center in Nairobi not only

trains local men, but has already trained meteorological officers from ten African countries outside the Community. The East African Telecommunications Central Training School, at Mbagathi in Kenya, teaches every aspect of communications. It also sponsors trainees for advanced courses for both local and overseas colleges, as does the Railway Training School in Kenya, and its sister school in Tanzania. And in 1968, the United Nations Development Program and the Community established a Staff Training College for both the railroad and harbor corporations.

The tremendous progress made by the Community's four corporations has excited outside interest and produced further offers of aid. The railroad's plan to add seventy diesel locomotives to its fleet brought a $13-million loan from the Canadian government with which to buy thirty-five of the locomotives from Canada and the remainder from Britain and West Germany. And the World Bank loaned some $38 million for relaying sections of railroads in Kenya.

The World Bank made a further $15 million available to the East African Posts and Telecommunications Corporation for extending the subscriber trunk-dialing system throughout the Community. And the three deep-water berths in Dar es Salaam's harbor was financed by a $34½-million loan from the World Bank.

A joint project of the United Nations Development program and the Community built a new school for the East African Directorate of Civil Aviation in Uganda where pilot training produces fifteen to twenty pilots and twenty aircraft maintenance engineers each year. Though the East African Airways Corporation has delivered expert service and has been the main overseas carrier, it has now started replacing its fleet of Comet-4's with DC-9's.

The visible evidence that three independent countries can

work together for their common benefit has aroused the interests of other East African countries who now seek entry into the Community which is always open for negotiation. Zambia, Ethiopia, Somalia, and Burundi are considering the possibilities of becoming member states. If their applications are acceptable to the Community, the degree of association will differ from one country to another. An expanded East African Community will be a tremendous forward step for a United States of Africa.

Ex-President Milton Obote sought refuge in Tanzania after the coup d'etat of January 25, 1971. His presence and the unsettled condition of Uganda created for a time an atmosphere of uncertainty and caution. Community employees became aware of the political implications of their decisions at the headquarters in Arusha. Could the Community continue to operate at the policy-making level, they wondered. Could the East African Authority still function with General Idi Amin? Though Mwalimu Nyerere said that he could not imagine transacting the business of the East African Authority with the general as the third party, Shafiq Arain, the general's friend, remained as Uganda's minister to the Community. Tensions were eased somewhat when in March, 1972, Milton Obote secretly left Tanzania for unknown parts—probably a country outside Africa.

The Community's three-year achievements tipped the scale in favor of carrying on as before, for the feeling of cooperation is deep and wide in East Africa. President Nyerere's driving ambition—cooperation—has become a way of life for 30 million East Africans. Though the experiment of working together has resumed, uncertainty and doubt as to the success or failure of the EAC will exist as long as there is border friction between Tanzania and Uganda.

16

The President Speaks

To introduce Tanzania's second Five-Year Plan at a TANU conference in Arusha in May, 1969, Mwalimu Nyerere welcomed the heads of state of neighboring countries. He drew attention to their mutual interests: ". . . Our brotherhood is a deep ocean of shared knowledge, mutual responsibilities, and interlocking affections. Those who wish to use us against each other, or to divide us from each other, should know that they are undertaking the task of drying up that ocean and blocking the rivers which feed it. . . ."

The president went on to outline the policies of the second Five-Year Plan which had been drawn up after close examination of the achievements and the failures of the first Five-Year Plan. Whereas the first plan took a major step toward a socialist state and served the people's own interests by improving living conditions for the peasant farmer, protecting the health of families and giving education to all children, the second plan aimed to be less rigid in application and with future predictions less precise. It would be more flexible, for the government would each year review the plan and make any necessary adjustments. The reviews would be called the *annual economic plans* and would be in connection with and affected by the annual budget.

The plan aimed to spread the benefits of development throughout society, encourage cooperative efforts, and avoid wide differences of wealth and income. It emphasized self-reliance by mobilizing the rural masses. And with "brotherhood" and the East African Community in mind, the president went on to stress that the plan was intended to be an extension of economic cooperation with other African states. The plan, filled with harmony and a hope for everlasting peace, was received joyously.

Yet two years later that "brotherhood" was threatened by dissension from within Africa at the annual Heads of State Conference of the Organization of African Unity. The OAU was formed in 1963, as an instrument to hold together new African states. At All-African summit meetings in OAU's spacious auditorium in Addis Ababa, Ethiopia, problems usually are settled amicably among African nations. But in June, 1971, an explosive political debate developed over whether or not to sanction the entering into trade relations with the Republic of South Africa.

Already, Malawi and Malagasy recognized the economic value of South Africa to them, and had dialogue with that country despite its race policy. Prior to the June meeting two new nations, Uganda and Central African Republic, expressed an interest in following their leads. They boycotted the meeting.

President Nyerere, adamant in his condemnation of a country with a minority white rule, stood firmly in opposition, and the Tanzanian government issued a pamphlet urging a reassessment of eligibility for OAU membership which, if adopted, would probably have excluded countries unwilling to continue their strong stands against South Africa.

Only a vote of twenty-seven was needed for adoption of a resolution that declares there is no basis for a meaningful dialogue with a minority racist regime. The crisis was reached and passed satisfactorily. At the final session of the summit meeting there were twenty-eight votes for adoption, six against, and five abstentions.

Problems arise within Tanzania also, and President Nyerere must keep a careful watch for conspiracies. One plot that failed was designed to overthrow the government and assassinate the president. Five political leaders and two army officers were among the traitors who planned to betray their country. One conspirator was Bibi Titi Mohammed who, as the former head of the Union of Tanzanian Women, worked with zest for Uhuru when Tanzania pressed for independence.

To forestall similar attempts and a military coup such as occurred in Uganda, Mwalimu Nyerere announced that the formation of a people's militia was necessary to guard the home front and to combat any foreign interference. The president was convinced that the ouster of President Obote of Uganda was the work of outsiders. At one rally he said, "We must now prepare ourselves for a confrontation with the imperialists. . . . From now on, the greatest task of the party and the army must be to teach our people how to fight."

Early in March, 1972, President Nyerere made drastic changes in his cabinet, his purpose being to strengthen leadership at the important rural level where problems are most likely to arise. He reduced the number of ministries from seventeen to sixteen, the Ministry for Rural Administration now being unnecessary since five former ministers were appointed to be additional regional commissioners with ministerial status, bringing their total to eighteen. They now serve on the TANU National Executive Committee, the major policy-making body in Tanzania.

A new post of prime minister was created and filled by Second Vice-President Rashidi Kawawa whose new duties include settling differences between ministers. All the new ministers are under forty. The youngest member of the new cabinet is Joseph Mungai, twenty-nine, appointed Minister of Agriculture. John Malecela (now Minister of Foreign Affairs) was at one time Tanzania's representative at the United Nations. Teachers are numbered among the new ministers. In 1965 the Rev. Simon Chiwanga (National Education) was a ringleader in a student demonstration against national service, and Daudi Mwakawago (Information and Broadcasting) has been principal of Kivukoni College, the political training school in Dar es Salaam. Two Masais are among the appointees. Edward Sokoine is now Minister of Defense, and Major-General Sarakikya, who was trained at Sandhurst in England, is head of the Tanzanian People's Defense Force.

Three ministers of the old cabinet were dropped entirely, one of whom was Derek Bryceson (former Minister of Agriculture), the last elected white minister in any of the new African nations.

Mwalimu Nyerere observes the principles of democratic socialism at all times. Rather than occupy the ostentatious State House in Dar es Salaam, he lives in an unpretentious suburban villa where Maria Nyerere devotes her days to their nine children, insisting on keeping them away from public attention. Nyerere spares one week each month, from writing articles, preparing speeches, and revising policies, to travel through the back coun-

President Nyerere on a visit to the cottage industries training center in Dar es Salaam, where he saw a bamboo-cutting machine and articles made from bamboo under the guidance of a Japanese expert.

try. He gives practical demonstrations to rural farmers, whether it is in the laying of bricks or the digging of ditches. And seeing their president work convinces the farmers more strongly that "Hard Work Is the Root of Development." Their sincerity and patriotism are evident when at rallies the farmers join in singing Tanzania's forceful national anthem:

> God bless Tanzania
> Grant eternal Freedom and
> Unity to its sons and
> daughters.
> God bless Tanzania
> and its people.
> Bless Tanzania
> Bless Tanzania
> Bless the children of
> Tanzania.

Which translated into Swahili reads:

> Mungu ibariki Tanzania
> Dumisha Uhuru na Umoja
> Wake Kwa Waume na
> Watoto.
> Mungu ibariki
> Tanzania na watu wake
> Ibariki Tanzania
> Ibariki Tanzania
> Tubariki Watoto wa
> Tanzania.

TANU party members are also inspired by the unceasing efforts of their tireless president. They are dedicated to nation-building and to living up to their party's pledge, which is:

I believe in the universal brotherhood of man and in the Unity of Africa.

I shall faithfully serve my country and its people.

I shall apply all my efforts toward the elimination of poverty, disease, ignorance, and corruption.

Corruption perverts justice; I shall neither offer nor accept bribes.

I shall never use my official position nor that of another person for my personal gain or private benefit.

I shall make available to the people of this country my knowledge and skill, which I shall constantly strive to advance.

I shall actively take part in the building of the Nation.

I shall always tell the truth and shall never bear any grudges against anybody.

I shall be a faithful member of TANU and a good citizen of Tanzania and Africa.

I shall be loyal to the President of the United Republic of Tanzania.

Index

Aboud Jumbe, 46
Addis Ababa, 129
African National Congress (ANC), 46
Afro-Shirazi party, 40, 42
Agriculture and Forestry Research Organization, 124
Alale, Pajume, 101
Amenital, 87, 88
Amin, General Idi, 120, 127
Angola, 80
Arabs, 20, 27, 40, 42
Arain, Shafiq, 127
Arusha, 18, 58, 111, 120, 128
Arusha Declaration, 50, 52, 54
Asians, 20, 42, 54

Babu, Abdulrahma, 50
Bagamoyo, 21, 40
Bantu, 24–27, 101
Beira, 82
Bibi Titi Mohammed, 34, 66, 130
British Anti-Slavery Society, 41
British Commonwealth of Nations, 14, 39

British Medical Research Council, 77
Bryceson, Derek, 131
Burite, Chief, 31
Burton, Sir Richard, 23
Burundi, 12, 127
Butiama, 31

Cairo, 18
Canada, 50
Cape Town, 18
Central Africa, 23
Central African Republic, 129
Central Secretariat, 120
Chagga, 64
Chinese, 42, 48, 83, 85, 94; Commission of Economic Affairs with Foreign Countries, 83
Chiwanga, Rev. Simon, 131
Common Market: Community Development (CD), 58–61, 63, 65; Council, 121, 122; Court of Appeals, 122; Tribunal, 122
Congo River, 13
Cooperatives, 63, 64

Corydon Museum, 24
Customs and Excise Department, 122
Czechoslovakia, 50

Dar es Salaam, 17, 18, 24, 34, 45, 48, 64, 77, 79–84, 88, 90, 102, 104, 118, 123
Daudi Mwakawago, 131
Department of Theater Arts, 99
Development Commission (DC), 61, 63
Directorate of Civil Aviation, 125
Dodoma, 18, 61, 77

East Africa, 11, 13, 22
East African (publishing company), 103
East African Airways Corporation, 119, 121, 126
East African Authority, 120, 127
East African Committee of Planners, 119
East African Community, 18, 118–120, 125, 127, 129
East African Development Bank, 122
East African Harbors Corporation, 121
East African Railways Corporation, 119, 121
East African Staff College, 125
East African Statistical Training Center, 125
East African Telecommunications Corporation, 121, 126
East African Telecommunications Central Training School, 126
East Germany, 42, 45
Edinburgh University, 32

Elizabeth, Queen, 97
Ethiopia, 127
Europeans, 20, 27, 29

Family Planning Association of Tanzania, 76
Fang-Yi, Mr., 83
Finance Council, 123
Five-Year-Plan, First, 47, 128; Second, 78, 128, 129
FRELIMO, 46
Freshwater Fisheries Research Organization, 124

German East Africa, 73
Gillman's Point, 117
Great Britain, 13
Great Lakes Region, 24
Great North Road, 18, 80
Great Rift Valley, 13

Hamites, 25

India, 23, 90
Indian Ocean, 11, 116
Industrial Shares Act, 54
Institute of Adult Education, 70, 104
Institute of Malaria and Vector-Borne Diseases, 123
Institute of Medical Research, 123
Institute of Swahili Research, 70
International Planned Parenthood, 77
International Red Cross, 48
Iringa, 80
Israel, 47
Italy, 90

Japan, 90

Kampala, 119, 120
Kapiri Mposhi, 85
Karema, 73
Karume, Sheikh Abeid A., 42–44, 46
Kaunda, President Kenneth, 83
Kawawa, Rashidi, 38, 44, 48, 50, 65, 92, 100, 131
Kenya, 12, 18, 23, 87, 119
Kilimanjaro Mountain Club, 117
Kisumu, 119
Kivukoni Training College, 61, 63, 66, 131
Kurasini, 83

Lakes: Manyara, 111; Nyasa, 12; Tanganyika, 12, 18, 73, 78; Victoria, 11, 18, 25, 31, 78, 88, 107, 119
Leakey, Dr. and Mrs. L. S. B., 24
Leprosy Research Center, 124
Livingstone, Dr. David, 73
Lusaka, 18, 79

Makerere University College, 32, 69
Makonde, 101, 102, 106
Malagasy, 129
Malawi, 12, 129
Malecela, John, 131
Marine Fisheries Research Organization, 124
Masai, 28, 63, 107
Mbeya, 18, 80, 91
McGill University, 95
Meteorological Training Center, 125
Meyer, Professor, 117
Mikumi, 80

Ministry of: Agriculture, 74; Health, 74, 77; Lands, Housing, and Urban Development, 61; National Culture, 98; Rural Administration, 130
Mnyampala, Mathias, 104
Morogoro, 18, 80
Moshi, 18, 64, 77
Mount Kibo, 117
Mount Kilimanjaro, 11, 18, 45, 50, 117, 118
Mozambique, 12, 18, 45, 50, 117, 118
Mtwara, 18, 80, 81, 90, 91
Mungai, Joseph, 131
Mwadui, 95
Mwakawago, Daudi, 131
Mwanza, 18, 64, 77, 87, 119
Mwanza Textile Company, 88
Mzee Kenyatta, 120

National Agricultural and Food Corporation (NAFCO), 54
National Agricultural and Forestry Research Organization, 124
National Arts of Tanzania, 101
National Development Corporation (NDC), 54, 55, 86, 87, 90–92, 95, 97, 101–103, 106, 114, 115
National Executive Committee, 131
Nationalist, The, 102, 104
National Service of Radio Tanzania, 104
National Small Industries Corporation, 91, 92
Ndola, 82
Ngorongoro Crater, 107
Nilo-Hamites, 27
Nsekela, Mrs. Christins, 77
"Nutcracker Man," 24

Nyanza Cooperative Union, 87
Nyerere, Burite, 31
Nyerere, Joseph, 104
Nyerere, Maria Gabriel, 33, 34, 131
Nyerere, President Julius Kambar-
  age, 31–40, 43, 44, 46–54, 57,
  58–71, 83, 86, 98, 103, 104, 120,
  127–131, 133, 134

Obote, Dr. Milton, 120, 127, 130
Observation Hill, 70
Okot p'Bitek, 103
Olduvai Gorge, 24
Operation Vijana, 104
Organization of African Unity
  (OAU), 129

Peace Corps, 49, 105
Peking, 48, 83
Pemba, 11, 13, 20, 41
"People's Education Plan," 65
People's Republic of China, 82, 92
Poland, 50
Portugal, Portuguese, 46

Railway Training School, 126
Region Development Fund, 63
Republic of South Africa, 46, 129
Revolutionary Council, 40, 42, 46
Rhodesia, 46, 80, 82
Royal Technical College, 69
Ruanda, 12
Rufiji Delta, 80, 85
Rural Health Clinics, 76
Russia, Russians, 42

Saint Francis School, 32
Sarakikya, Major-General, 131
Sayyid Said, Imam of Oman, 41

Serengeti, 107
Shirazi, 41
Sokoine, Edward, 131
Somalia, 127
Songambele, Coast Regional Com-
  missioner, 104
Songea, 64
Southern Highlands, 18, 84, 85
Southwest People's Organization
  (SWAPO), 46
Speke, John, 23
Standard, The, 102, 104
Sudan, 25
Sukuma, Sukumaland, 25
Sunnite Arabs, 41
Swahili, 22, 65–67, 102, 103, 133
Sweden, 79

Tabora, 18, 32, 93, 96
Tanga, 17, 61, 92, 104
Tanganyika, 15
Tanganyika African Association
  (TAA), 32
Tanganyika African National Union
  (TANU), 32–37, 50–57, 66, 69,
  105, 128, 134
Tanganyika Packers Company, 91
TANU Youth League (TYL), 66, 76,
  104
Tanzam (Tanzania-Zambia road),
  80, 82, 91
Tanzania (name), 14, 15
Tanzania Broadcasting Company
  (TBC), 65, 66
Tanzania Dance Company (TDC),
  100
Tanzania Diamond Cutting Com-
  pany, 95

Tanzania Diamond Sorting Organization, 95
Tanzania National Transport Corporation, 82
Tanzania Portland Cement Company, 92, 94
Tanzania Tourist Board, 114, 117
Tanzanian People's Defense Force, 131
Tanzanian Publishing House, Ltd., 103
Tanzara (Tanzania-Zambia Railroad), 82–85, 91
Tarangire Park, 111
Tengoru College, 58
Treaty for East African Cooperation, 120
Tropical Pesticides Institute, 123
Trypanosomiasis Research Organization, 124
Tuberculosis Research Center, 124
Tunduma, 80

Ubungo Farm Implement Manufacturing Company, 92
Uganda, 12, 18, 119, 120, 129
Uhuru Point, 117
Ujamaa villages, 56, 58–63, 66, 86, 91, 106
Ujiji, 21
Unilateral Declaration of Independence (Rhodesia), 82
United Nations, 36, 37, 82, 131; Children's Fund (UNICEF), 48, 74; Development Program, 126; Food and Agricultural Organization, 74; Trusteeship, 13
United Republic Army, 50

United Republic of Tanzania, 11, 14, 43, 46
United Republic Parliament, 47
United States of Africa, 127
United States of America, 47, 54, 79, 82
United Women of Tanganyika (UWT), 34, 35
University College, 69, 70, 72
University of Dar es Salaam, 70, 94, 98, 104
Usambara Highlands, 92

Veterinary Research Organization, 124
Virus Research Institute, 124

Wazanaki tribe, 31
West Germany, 47, 50, 66
White Nile River, 12
Wildlife, 18, 107–117
Williamson Company Ltd., 95
Williamson, Dr. John T., 95–97
World Bank, 82, 126
World Health Organization (WHO), 77

Zaire (formerly the Congo), 12
Zambezi River, 13
Zambia, 12, 18, 79, 80, 82–84, 94, 96, 127
Zanzibar, 11, 13, 15, 20, 40–46, 51, 54, 123
Zanzibar and Pemba People's party (ZPPP), 42
Zimbabwe African National Union (ZANU), 46
Zinjanthropus, 24

About the Author

Edna Mason Kaula was born in Australia and was graduated from the Sydney Technical College. She has lived in Java, New Zealand, Holland, and Rhodesia, and has visited several of the Pacific Islands and much of Europe and the Middle East. Mrs. Kaula spent the year 1953 on a ranch in East Africa and returned there for subsequent visits, during which she stayed in small villages and spoke with everyone from tobacco growers to Bantu chiefs, thus gaining a firsthand knowledge of East Africa and its people.

Mrs. Kaula is the author of four more books in this series, THE LAND AND PEOPLE OF ETHIOPIA, THE LAND AND PEOPLE OF KENYA, THE LAND AND PEOPLE OF NEW ZEALAND, and THE LAND AND PEOPLE OF RHODESIA. She is also a painter and illustrator. She is now a citizen of the United States and lives in Providence, Rhode Island.